THE
SPARKLES
IN ME

JORETTA LUREE VETOR

ISBN: 1722408529
ISBN-13: 978-1722408527

Pulpit to Page Publishing Co. books may be ordered through booksellers or by contacting:
Pulpit to Page Publishing Co.
Warsaw, Indiana
pulpittopage.com

DEDICATION

I dedicate this book to my sons, Trenton, my Superman, and Dakota, my Warrior. Thank you to my husband, Darrell, my fortress.

I do want to also thank Steve Leer! Without his encouragement, this would have taken so much longer. I also want to mention Nick Poe for the guidance and assistance in the publication of this book — thank you!

...Remember it only takes one moment, one spark, to flicker into life and open up a child's world forever. Never stop looking for that spark.

CONTENTS

Foreword   6

The Sparkles in Me Poem   7

Preface   15

Sparkle Thoughts for Adults   18

Why Color is Important   30

The Rainbow   33

The Gingerbread Man   35

The Stack Up Game   43

Alphabet Chart   51

Emotional Instruction   56

Visualizing   63

Stories (for all colors)   65

Charts and Resources   179

My Story   188

Final Thoughts   193

Real Life Example   198

FOREWORD

TESTIMONIAL & INTRODUCTION

We had taken a foster child into our home and loved her as our own child. But as years passed, we realized that our love wasn't making a connection to Elisa's heart. Her inner turmoil was being acted out with aggression. I cried to the Lord for wisdom and He gave me JoRetta.

The colors appealed to Elisa immediately and drew out communication that she had buried because she had no vocabulary to express it. Together, we have learned how to share hurts and emotions in a non-threatening way. Colors are everywhere as a constant reminder that we are loved and a family.

I've been able to introduce this unique and effective communication tool to other families who are in a recovery program. In a God given way, it has been a bridge to emotional healing. Thank you!

—Donna Rhoades

THE SPARKLES IN ME

POEM

As STRONG as the Lion
as MIGHTY as can be

I have the SPARKLE
of **RED** in me.

As WISE as the owl
as QUIET as can be

I have the SPARKLE
of **ORANGE** in me

As BRIGHT as the sun
as SMART as can be

I have the SPARKLE
of YELLOW in me

As CALM as the grass
as KIND as can be

I have the SPARKLE
of GREEN in me

As DEEP as the ocean
as TRUE as can be

I have the SPARKLE
of **BLUE** in me

As DREAMY as the heavens
as PRAYER can be

I have the SPARKLE
of **PURPLE** in me

THE SPARKLES IN ME

P O E M

As STRONG as the Lion
as MIGHTY as can be
I have the SPARKLE
of **RED** in me.

As WISE as the owl
as QUIET as can be
I have the SPARKLE
of ORANGE in me

As BRIGHT as the sun
as SMART as can be
I have the SPARKLE
of YELLOW in me

As CALM as the grass
as KIND as can be
I have the SPARKLE
of GREEN in me

As DEEP as the ocean
as TRUE as can be
I have the SPARKLE
of **BLUE** in me

As DREAMY as the heavens
as PRAYER can be
I have the SPARKLE
of **PURPLE** in me

SPARKLE POWER WORDS

POWER
SELF CONTROL
BE HEALTHY
PHYSICAL STRENGTH
ENERGY
WISDOM
COURAGE
PATIENCE
RESPECT
BELONGING
LEARNING
CONFIDENCE
SHIFTING MY WILL
FEEL EMOTIONS
HOPE
KINDNESS
PEACE
HAPPINESS
LOVE
CALMNESS
TELL THE TRUTH
HAVE FAITH
WATCH MY WORDS
ASK FOR HELP
KNOW TRUE THINGS
PRAYER
CREATE
IMAGINATION
TRUST GOD
DREAMS

PREFACE

How do I help you change your world? Do you struggle to communicate to your child? Is your relationship chaotic and a battle of wills? Do you want better communication with your child, less chaos, fewer daily battles of will in your home? Do you want to be able to see into your child in a more meaningful way, and understand them better than you do now? Are you frustrated that you can't do more to help them? Is there an area in your child's life that you just wish they did not have to struggle with so much? How would you help them if you could? What would you do differently to have a better relationship with your child, or your students, or your clients?

What if I told you that you are about to change the way you look at your child, their world, and your world, forever? What if I told you the answer is so simple and it has been right in front of you all along, and that it could even improve your relationship with others you come in contact with everyday?

If you are reading this book of tools, it's probably because you are looking for something new and have exhausted all options in your search for answers. Maybe you're tired of your heart being broken by systems of professional "therapy" and empty promises. Maybe you have spent much, much money on counseling, and other conventional "treatments" and come away with little more than a lighter wallet. Perhaps those treatments have left you and your child only frustrated, and possibly have made matters worse! Maybe nothing has worked and you are grieving for your child who is locked in their own world, and for yourself, who has to stand on the outside of that thick glass wall, and all you can do is watch from the outside. You may be desperate.

I've been where you are. I was desperate to communicate with my own son when he was a boy all those years ago. It was out of that a motherly desperation to connect with him that *The Sparkles In Me* was born.

I developed the Sparkles communication system over 30 years ago. In the years that have followed I've taught it to parents, children and care givers of all kinds.

Maybe things are not that bad and you are just looking for a more meaningful way to get into your child's world, no matter how old they are. Maybe you are tired of ways to communicate only being taught from the perspective that a child cannot grasp it without being 'instructed' to learn a specific way of communicating. By the same token, maybe you are tired of some therapy or counseling methods being dumbed down so your child can correctly answer a questionnaire, but it doesn't REALLY say who YOUR child is.

The Sparkles In Me is not just a system of communication, it is a lifestyle. I can help you change your world. I can help you change the daily life of your children. With *The Sparkles In Me* incorporated into your daily life, life is about to get, and stay, a lot more fun and interesting. It is tried and tested. It works.

There is light at the end of the tunnel. A light that leads to hope.

The Sparkles In Me will lead you there.

SPARKLE THOUGHTS

FOR ADULTS

RED

"Alert!" "Stop!" "Warning!" "Danger!" Powerful, invigorating, vivacious, high energy, life-source, Blood. These are words we automatically associate with the color Red. Red invokes action and usually some form of physical response. It invokes our physical strength.

A red firetruck or ambulance racing by reminds us that every second counts in an emergency. The symbol of the Red Cross represents urgent care and aid... Immediate reaction.

Our Red Sparkle energy resonates in our lowest core. For children I tell them to imagine where their tail would be if they were a lion, We feel our Red Sparkle mostly in our arms, hand, legs and feet. As my poem says, "As strong as the lion. As mighty as can be. I have the Sparkle of RED in me."

When our Red Sparkle is too small or 'out of place', we can let our hands and feet get us into trouble. We kick things or hit people. When our Red Sparkle is bright and big, and in its proper place, we are poised and in control.

We have self-control. Think of the mighty Lion. The King of the jungle. The lion has to do nothing to be powerful, but breathe. By just being alive, the lion commands respect. How majestic is the male lion! It is a universal symbol of power.

"I just saw red!'" We have all heard that as the reason someone lashed out in anger. If you or your child is having a problem with anger and lashing out, try this for two weeks: Put a picture of a male lion up on the fridge. Or make it the background picture on your phone.

Keep it somewhere where you will see if often. It will be a helpful tool to remind you of your quiet, stately, healthy power, and that to have that power all you have to do is breathe. No need to go lashing out and acting all crazy.

The sound of the roar of a male lion is very distinctive. It's one of my favorite sounds. We are reminded in Isaiah 31:4 and Revelation 5:5 of that lion's powerful presence and fearlessness. Jesus portrayed as the Lion of Judah is one of my favorite images.

Infuse Red into your life. Notice the things around you that make you "see red" and think of yourself as the mighty lion, needing to do nothing to have power in the situation but to stand still and breathe. Need power? Eat red foods (Be careful of allergies to red dye in foods) Feeling sluggish, wear something red. Need to be more alert on the job? Keep a small red dot of some kind, (drawing etc.) somewhere at work where you see if often. It will help you stay energized.

ORANGE

There is nothing like the smell of a fresh orange. I remember getting an orange for Christmas in my stocking. That still makes me smile.

Our Orange Sparkle energy resonates just below our belly button. Our gut. Orange invokes wisdom. It is that 'gut feeling' you get, and should follow. That 'gut feeling' that a lot of the time is immediate and can defy logic. But it's so important. As my poem says, "As wise as the owl. As quiet as can be. I have the Sparkle of Orange in me."

A clear sky sunset is a good time to think about and have conversation about Orange. During a sunset, you can talk about, "Did you go with your gut today?" "Were you wise in your decisions today?" "Did you listen to or inspire wisdom?"

Just as Orange spans across the horizon at sunset, strive to let Wisdom span across your life. It will require correct choices, and being willing to be still at times to let Wisdom permeate a situation. To "Be still and know" requires practice, practice, practice. It isn't always easy, but is necessary if you want to live a more peaceful, wise and less dramatic life.

The orange fruit makes me think of Vitamin C, which makes me think of good health. Good digestion is essential to good health. All good health.

The next time you hold an orange in your hands, or see an orange flower growing in the wild, take a moment to think about wisdom, quiet, purposeful Wisdom and how rare it truly is. Infuse Orange into your life on purpose. Have an important decision to make? Tie an orange string around your wrist. Eat orange foods. Grow pumpkins.

YELLOW

Most of us when we think of the color Yellow think of a big bright yellow Sun. Yellow invokes happiness and promotes a good mood. It invokes learning. Our Yellow Sparkle energy resonates in just above our belly button, the diaphragm, and in our nerves.

As my poem says, "As bright as the Sun, as smart as can be. I have the Sparkle of Yellow in me." I believe it sits between your 'knowing' of orange and your 'choosing' of green. Yellow invokes learning and education, healthy self-pride, accomplishment, emotional satisfaction. Happiness. Joy. Confidence. This is so important.

We often overlook or downplay this, especially in our children. Learning and mastering new things brings confidence. This takes patience. In our fast-paced world, we are losing how to truly master anything and to take pride in it.

Yellow invokes Hope. Start paying attention to how it makes you feel that moment sunshine breaks through on a cloudy day. When you need to lift your spirits wear something yellow, turn on a pale yellow light in your home or light a candle. I so love the soft yellow gold of a candle's flame.

I once read that one can see a single candle light glowing from a mile away if everything else is total darkness. That's powerful. Hope in the darkness. Psalms 68:13 reminds us that we are like doves with silver wings, tipped in yellow gold. I like that.

GREEN

Why is the earth covered with green grass and trees with green leaves? Why green instead of any other color or color combination? Peace. Heart. Love. Serenity. Kindness. Calmness. Our Green Sparkle energy resonates in our heart. As my poem says, "As calm as the grass. As kind as can be. I have the Sparkle of Green in me."

Think about laying back in a field of tall green grass. As a little girl that was one of my favorite things to do. The grass was so high that it hid me from the rest of the world. It was peaceful. The grass smelled so good. Looking up at the big, cottony clouds floating by and imagining the pictures of shapes they formed just for me. When I am stressed, I still lie down in a field of grass and breath it in.

We take a drive or walk out to the county to get away from stress, to take a break for our hurried lives, and to 'get back to nature'. Even the phrase, 'get back to nature' reminds us of where we belong and how we belong there. 'To be in tune with nature' is another familiar phrase. Why?

Green invokes love, kindness, calmness, decision making, choosing. We want the desires of our heart, not the desires of our big toe. There's a reason for that.

What is your passion? What lies so deep in your heart that nothing could persuade you to go against it? How careful are you with your heart, both literally and figuratively? Do you take good care of your heart? Are you careful of your choosing? Do your choices give you peace?

"Matters of the heart" are just that. The green sparkle energy that resonates within our heart gets pumped like our blood through our whole being. If we can be more aware of how green affects our being, and look for it more, notice it more in our world around us, the better choices we will make and the calmer we will be.

Infuse green into your life on purpose. It's our 'being thankful place' in our soul. Remind yourself to be thankful. It's good for your heart.

BLUE

Our days begin and end with Truth. This thought occurred to me one day as I was watching the twilight blue sky of night turning into day. It's such a mystical color. It's an indescribable color. Black, darkest navy blue, azure turns into a quickest hint if neon blue, just as the palest sweetest yellow bridges upon the horizon. The Blues of Truth, God's calm, steady, quiet Truth welcomes a new day.

And the last color we see, after the mural of the sunset? The last color that hangs in the sky before nightfall? Blue. The same mystical blues, that started the day slowly covered the sky to end the day. A thought trickled through my mind, that no matter what had happened in the world during the day, God had begun and ended it with perfect, deep, quietness of Truth. Our happenings and our world may not be relevant to another person's world, but God sees it all. His ways are not our ways. When I think of the moment the day begins and the moment the day ends, and look up at the sky in those Blue moments, it helps to put things in perspective. How grand is the twilight.

Look up. Keep your head up. How often do we hear that? But, really, when you look up into the sky on a bright and sunny clear day, what do you see? Blue. Quiet Truth just being there. A constant reminder to " BE still and know…" If we would just pay attention. We don't have to do anything on our part to make a blue sky a blue sky. Just lift your face toward the sun and soak it into you mind and heart.

Water. As my poem says, "as deep as the ocean, as true as the sea, I have the sparkle of Blue in Me." Truth is in us. Think of deep, blue rivers, lakes, oceans,. Water. Life is running water. Have you ever wondered why it is water that all living things have to have to survive? Why is most of the earth covered in water? Why is a cool wet cloth on a child's feverish forehead so soothing for them? Water.

Think of water as Truth. Water, just by the virtue of its being, is one of the more powerful forces on earth. Nothing stands in the path of a hurricane to prevent it from coming. Creeks and rivers eventually and amazingly find their way through obstacles as they continue to flow. Rain, Tears, Snow, Ice, Steam. You can see Truth there if you want to. How comforting and restful is a hot bath? Or a cool dip in the pool of water?

Our Blue Sparkle of energy resonates in our throat. When we speak or hear truth we subconsciously know it. When we are about to say something important, we may instinctively "clear our throat" Why? To make way for Truth. When we say someone is 'true blue', we mean they are honest.

When you need to clear your head or take time to think, get to a place where there is water like a river, stream, lake, ocean, etc. If you can't do that, purposefully eat foods that are blue, like blueberries, carry a blue stone in your pocket, or wear a piece of blue clothing. Plant blue flowers in your garden. Put a blue dot on the back of your hand, or on your wrist to help you use your Blue Sparkle when Truth is something on your mind. It will help you own your own Truth and get more comfortable with it. This is so important. Change the conversation in your head from, "Is that a lie?" to " Where is the Blue in that?" And with your children, from "Why did you lie?" to "What is the Blue truth answer?" You may see Truth come more quickly and easily.

Infuse Blue into your life. One of my favorite verses is Philippians 4:8 Finally, brethren, whatsoever things are true, whatsoever things are honest, whatsoever things are just, whatsoever things are pure, whatsoever things are lovely whatsoever things are of good report; if there be any virtue, and if there be any praise, think on these things.

I always think of the Blue twilight morning and evening sky when I come across this verse.

PURPLE

Purple just fascinates me. Again, go to the early sunrise and late sunset. How often do you witness these quiet and powerful events and think "How majestic!" And it is. Purple represents royalty, majesty and spiritual connection and God puts it in the sky for us every day.

Our Purple Sparkle energy resonates in our brains, our 'third eye', our mind. There is a reason the phrase 'peace of mind' is what it is. We feel something is settled when it gives us peace of mind. Purple invokes our highest thought, our dreams, our prayers, our subconscious and our imagination. It invokes our connection to our spiritual self and to God.

Every single thing that has been made by man started with a thought, an idea. I always tell my children that "Thoughts are things!" What we focus our thoughts on eventually comes into our reality. Think about that.

Having trouble with a project, or thinking something through and you need inspiration? Infuse purple into your life on purpose. See purple as a wonderment for all it represents. Jesus said, "My peace I leave with you." John 14:27. Oh, if we could really grasp that. One could spend their whole life just contemplating on that verse. And we should.

During hard times, and I have had and do have plenty, I remind myself of Philippians 4:8. It's powerful. It doesn't say it is easy to do.

And I will admit there have been some pretty low times in my life when I couldn't even get to the part of thinking about those things the verse encourages us to think about. All I could do was just keep reminding myself the verse was there for a reason. Over and over and over.

Our thoughts are so important. They become our daily life. You've heard the phrase, 'garbage in-garbage out'. Well, yeah. What you put into your brain, literally and figuratively, will become evident in your physical world. For all the world to see. We must remember that we are just passing through this world. My home is in heaven. I think of Jesus being there. As my poem says, " As dreamy as the heavens, as prayers can be, I have the Sparkle of Purple in me."

All physical aspects of our being started out as spiritual issue or knowing and then became a thought, which ended up a physical thing.

Infuse Purple into your life on purpose. Think the highest and best thoughts., Guard your mind and the wonders that are within it. Think royally. You are a child of the Most High King after all. Wear purple. Plant purple flowers in your garden. Need a hug? Wear something purple and remind yourself of the royalty that you are.

WHY COLOR

IS IMPORTANT

Why is the grass green? Why is the sky blue? Why are rainbow colors the rainbow colors?

Why is sunshine yellow? Why are storm clouds dark and gray and almost black? Why is a beautiful sunset streamed with so many different colors and you cannot tell where one ends and the next begins? Color used correctly must be pretty important to God and the whole universe.

Green promotes a feeling of calm and of well-being. We take a walk out to the country or go to a park to relax and calm down, to unwind and breathe deep. Could you imagine, do you think you would get the same feelings if the grass was all different color polka dots?

Blue causes one to be reflective, as many paintings of rivers and oceans can attest to. We go to the water to sit and think. We return from a beach vacation regrouped and revitalized.

Yellow makes us happy. Just think of how many times you have turned your face toward a bright shining sun, felt the its warmth and that simply made you smile.

See where I am going here? God knew which colors were supposed to be where and how to use them. He gave us the same power, and knowledge and peace about colors. We just have to learn how to use it in our daily lives.

COLOR WAVES

The visible light spectrum is part of the electromagnetic spectrum and its wavelengths range from approximately from 380 to 740 nanometers (nm). Science proves this.

Color is a wave traveling through space. Depending on the wavelength, the space between the peaks – measured in nanometers nm – is registered by our eyes as different colors.

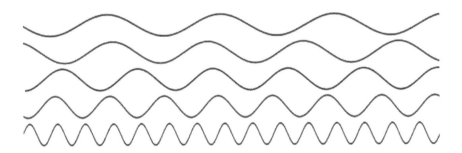

Sine Wave is the measurement of energy, used to depict frequency, vibration, and waves. It is a waveform, a single frequency repeated indefinitely in time.

THE VISIBLE LIGHT SPECTRUM

Color	Wavelength (nm)	Frequency THz
Red	625 - 740	400 - 484
Orange	590 - 625	484 - 508
Yellow	565 - 590	508 - 526
Green	520 - 565	526 - 606
Blue	500 - 520	606 - 670
Indigo	435 - 500	670 - 700
Violet	380 - 435	700 - 789

THE RAINBOW

Have you ever wondered why the rainbow is in the sky? Why, really? Just seeing a rainbow makes us feel good. There have been many things attached to the meaning of the colorful band in the sky. From Bible stories to groups of people, we want to claim our reason for why the rainbow means something to us. There is a reason why we want to identify with it. It makes perfect sense that we want to identify with the rainbow. It is truly a thing of fascination and wonder.

Scientifically simple in its explanation, the rainbow is all of the colors separated by light. For me, the reason for the rainbow is equally as simple. It reminds us of who we are, broken down in simple terms, piece by piece, color by color. How marvelous!

The whole premise of The Sparkles In Me is that God sees us perfectly. Imagine God looking down from heaven at a rainbow. He sees clear through it. He sees it from his perspective. I believe God sees us as one looks down onto a prism. Like a perfect crystal. If you are standing above the prism and you look straight down through it, you only see crystal clear prism. No separation of colors. Perfection.

When we look up at a rainbow in the sky, we see separated colors. We see it from our perspective of being on the ground. Looking at a prism is the same. It is only when we look at the prism in a way other than from above it, that we see separated colors. Think of this the next time you see a rainbow. It is a perfect opportunity to have a Sparkles conversation with your child.

THE GINGERBREAD MAN

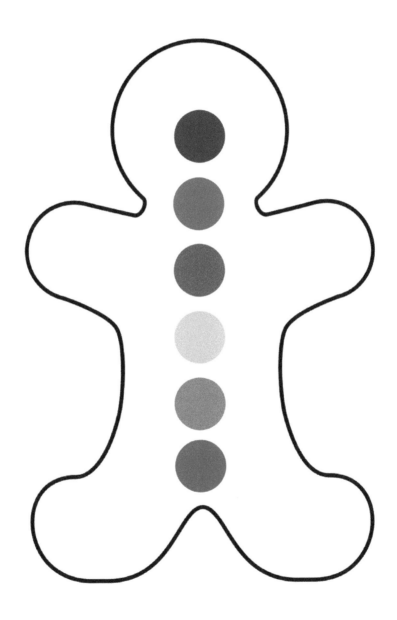

PHOTOCOPY VERSION

THE GINGERBREAD MAN

EXPLAINED

The Gingerbread Man is the symbol for the communication we use in *The Sparkles in Me*. It is the window into your child's mind and soul. With practice, you will be able to understand what your child is not telling you out loud. There are no wrong answers when they draw on their Gingerbread Man. The colors each represent a specific thing that your child will be communicating. We'll get into that later.

To start, keep a picture of the Gingerbread Man with his Sparkle colors stacked up neatly inside of him, in a place where your child will see if it often. When you have your Sparkle time together and you are going to use the Gingerbread Man, **ALWAYS** have your child color in the correct Sparkle colors in the correct places before you move on to anything else. Why? Because God sees us perfectly. This is how we are made. God always sees us first in perfect order. You do not have to explain this every time to your child. But, keep gently reminding them that FIRST God always sees them as perfect.

This is so important. This is the perfect place from where your child starts. The Sparkles In Me way of communication says, "You are already perfect, healed, obedient, and so forth. We just have to help you remember *who you really are*." Keep your explanation simple. It gives your child a foundation of acceptance, confidence and trust. Especially when you say things like, "See this Gingerbread Man? This is how I see the real you, too."

As you color in each Sparkle color inside the Gingerbread man, go over what each color means and where it is in your child's body. Keep it simple. This gives your child an opportunity to talk about each color. This builds communication. Some children see their Sparkles as a shield that they can stand behind. Some see them as bubbles inside themselves. Some see them as that whole body part. There are no wrong answers. Pay attention to how your child sees the Sparkle colors inside themselves.

Good Day/Bad Day

Next comes the good day/bad day game. This changes "How does that make your feel?" to "Where is your Sparkles color about that?" This will inspire communication!

Start with their Gingerbread Man colored correctly, then give your child a blank Gingerbread Man page they are going to color in. Start with RED. You Point to the RED Sparkle and say, "On a good day, (whatever your subject of of discussion is: school, dealing with siblings, minding your manners, etc.) your RED is here, like a mighty strong lion. You are in control of your body." Then give your child a red writing utensil. "So, on a bad day, where do you Feel your RED?" Let your child draw on the blank Gingerbread Man. They will draw on him where they feel their red on a bad day, even if it is outside of the Gingerbread Man. (And doesn't that speak volumes?)

You then follow through with all of the colors.

"On a good day, your ORANGE is here (pointing to the ORANGE Sparkle), sitting like a wise old owl, making good decisions." Then give your child an orange writing utensil. "So, on a bad day, where do you feel your ORANGE?"

"On a good day, your YELLOW is here, learning new things and feeling good about yourself." Then give your child a yellow writing utensil. "So on a bad day, where is your yellow?"

"On a good day, your GREEN is here, and your heart is happy and full of good things that you do." Then give your child a green writing utensil. "So on a bad day, where is your green?"

"On a good day, your BLUE is here, and you tell the truth and you know when you hear the truth. You are proud of your truth words that you say." Then give your child a blue writing utensil. "So on a bad day, where is your blue?"

"On a good day, your PURPLE is here, full of great imagination, hopes, dreams, prayers, and creative things you want to do." Then give your child a purple writing utensil. "So on a bad day, where is your purple?"

I suggest your keep these Gingerbread Man papers and date them. This will show your child's progress. I have found that a child likes to see their papers that show how they have learned to handle themselves better in any area. For example, maybe in the beginning on a bad day, their RED was scribbled all throughout over their whole Gingerbread Man (and really it means they felt that angry in their whole entire body!) You show them that paper. And as they have continued to incorporate The Sparkles In Me into their life, they now draw RED only in the Gingerbread Man's head – or leg if they kicked their sibling that week.

I love to see their eyes light up when they see the Gingerbread Man papers side by side and realize how they have changed! Again, this is an opportunity for communication! Remember there are no wrong answers as they draw their Sparkles. It is always an opportunity for communication to begin. Be patient.

Essentially, this practice simply helps a child communicate emotion through very easy means... like colors and drawing. They learn to "hide" behind, or inside of, their sparkles. It is safe there. It is a safe place to talk about their emotions, etc. Keep it a safe place for your child. Remember, try not to lead your child into answer. Just listen to them. There are no wrong answers.

QUICK TIPS

FOR USING THE
GINGERBREAD MAN

- Make gingerbread man cookies.
- Put a picture of a correctly colored in gingerbread man in your child's room.
- Switch the writing utensils; don't use the same type all the time.
- Color in the Sparkle colors and leave one out, and tell your child the left out color is the one the two of you are going to work on that day.
- Let your child pick what color they want to work on.
- The Christmas season is a great time to find gingerbread man decorations, coloring books, children's books, etc.
- Make your child a Sparkle colors blanket or pillow in the gingerbread man shape.
- Let your child name their gingerbread man.

THE STACK-UP GAME

FIRST LINE OF

COMMUNICATION

How many times do you hear yourself say to your child, "Just be still! Stop it! Calm down! Be still!" And how frustrating does that get for all involved?

With using *The Sparkles In Me* and the STACK UP GAME, you can teach your child how to be still and control themselves, on their own, without fighting and yelling and wearing both of you out.

We are designed by our Creator to be calm, have our minds at ease, and to love. I am so tickled that science is now catching up and proving this concept. Could you imagine God up in heaven shouting and shaking His finger at you, and getting frustrated with you because you couldn't sit still? I don't think so. God's way of thinking is always to lead us to calm. (GREEN SPARKLE)

But how do we show our child that they already have this ability inside them? We simply remind them, as many times as it takes, who they really are. They are perfection.

We teach them to use their GREEN Sparkle. It is the same with each Sparkle color and the powers and abilities that go with them.

If you have ever had a child who had a meltdown in a grocery store, you can relate to a certain kind of parent panic. Whatever the reason for the meltdown, the acting out can be nerve wracking. And in most cases, if your child has reached meltdown status, they cannot communicate to you what is really going on inside them emotionally. They cannot tell you what is really making them upset.

Sometimes they are too tired, or hungry. Sometimes they are just having a temper tantrum. But communicating to your child that it is time to "STACK UP," and doing it with them as you need to, you'll see a calmer and rational child emerge more quickly.

Remember this is not punishment and should never be presented as such. Nothing in **The Sparkles in Me** is meant to be implemented as a punishment. Your voice and how you speak to your child matters immensely.

No cheating. Do the STACK UP properly, color by color. Start over as many times as you need to until your child has their colors all stacked up. This is accomplishment! This is a good thing.

By visualizing the Sparkles stacked up one on top of the other, in their proper order, your child will learn to calm and steady themselves. This is such a great life skill to have!

As my children grew and we used this technique, I could see it working and was amazed. I could actually see their posture change when they "stacked up." And with repetition, they could calm themselves quicker and quicker.

Pay attention. If you see your child hesitate or refuse on stacking up a color, it may be an opportunity to have a talk about the things color is associated with as it pertains to the Sparkles in your child. Playing the STACK UP GAME will help you understand what is going on with your child emotionally, and that is what this communication is all about: helping them.

I'll tell you a funny little story to help illustrate the point, based on a child stacking up his colors.

While grocery shopping with one of my sons (he was about six years old), I noticed a toy had "mysteriously" found its way into my shopping cart. When I asked my son how the toy got there, he shrugged his little shoulders and said, "I don't know." The game was on.

He had a problem with telling lies. (He won't mind me sharing this.) And he was a good liar. The kid had it down to an art form. So if I let one lie go, things would soon snowball out of control, he would display his temper, etc.

Even though we were in the grocery store, the mysteriously appearing toy had to be dealt with. So right there in the middle of the aisle we started to play the STACK UP GAME. He knew the poem by heart, so all I had to do was have him say the colors and do the hand placements. He was not happy about it! Because of his stubbornness, just getting him to put his hands on his hips and say "RED" took about ten minutes. But I was not going to let him lose this battle with his temper and emotions. We could spend all day at the grocery as far as I was concerned.

He got to the color blue and he would not say the word or do the hand placement. He skipped blue and went right to purple, with a sweet smile. It was hard for me to keep a straight face! So we started over many times. I peeled a banana and had a snack while we waited for him to choose to stack up all of his Sparkles. I paid for the eaten banana. Finally, after a good twenty minutes, he took a deep, dramatic breath and stacked up all of his colors, quickly and correctly. In that moment I was a proud mamma.

Then he suddenly fell to the ground and didn't move! Scared me half to death! I ran to his side and picked him up. I asked him, "Hunny! Hunny! Are you okay? What happened?"

He looked up at me and said, "My BLUE fell out!" His BLUE Sparkle fell out of the stack he was seeing in his mind and 'made him fall down.' I knew he was saying to me that he could not bring himself to tell me the truth about slipping the toy into the shopping cart while I wasn't looking. We had progress!

The solution was to start over stacking up his Sparkles. But when he got to blue, he could put the toy back on the shelf and say "BLUE" at the same time. This way BLUE was acknowledged, and it paved an easier way for him to tell the truth. At the checkout, I let him get a blue piece of candy as a reward.

Celebrate even the smallest victories.

Hand Placements and How to Start the STACK UP GAME

The STACK UP GAME is key to the communication that *The Sparkles In Me* is all about. You play the STACK UP GAME by using the hand placements as you say *The Sparkles In Me* poem. By using the hand placements, your child will associate the Sparkle colors with where they are in their own body. This STACK UP GAME *is your building block for everything else in communication.*

If you are in a sit-down session, at the beginning of every Sparkle time you have with your child, start with the STACK UP GAME. (After this, you bring out the Gingerbread Man. The Gingerbread Man is explained in a separate section of this book.)

This is key! If you stick with this formula, you will see results in your child faster than you ever could have imagined! As you incorporate *The Sparkles In Me* into your life, as with any thing, the more you do it, the easier it gets. The great thing about the STACK UP GAME is you can do it almost anywhere and at any time. Do not demand that your child "stack up" like they are being punished. If you do that you are missing the whole point. It's a game. Your child can be sitting or standing. Start with RED. Ask your child to dig their RED claws, like a lion, deep into the ground. They will see this in their imagination. Digging their "claws" into the ground helps them stay in one spot.

Next, have them put their hands on their hips and say "RED." (They can wiggle their hips and pretend to have a lion's tail.) Ask your child to let you know when their RED Sparkle is in place so they can go on to the next color. Then, one by one, tell them to put the next color on top of the last color and to let you know when they have done that.

Pay attention. Don't rush your child. If they believe you see their Sparkle colors stacking up like they see them, you are building a bond – a bond of trust and communication. By the time they put their PURPLE Sparkle in their head, you will probably see a difference in your child's demeanor.

Repetition is key! Practice the STACK UP GAME often when your child is not upset. Play with colored blocks. Make it a game. Then when it is crunch time – such as the grocery store meltdown – your child will be more confident to stack up their Sparkles colors that are inside of them. Be your child's best advocate. Help them help themselves. When you know your child is getting close to a meltdown, or is about to do something that usually gets them into trouble, ask them if they want to take a minute and STACK UP. Tell them to use their Sparkles.

It is easier for a child to concentrate on a color than on a concept. The concepts will follow in time, and you may be amazed at what you and your child both learn. I believe it is never too young to start.

Repetition matters, even to a newborn baby.

ALPHABET CHART

A B C D E F G H I J K L M N O P Q R
S T U V W X Y Z
a bc de f gh i jk l mn o pq rs t u v wx
y z
ch ing silent 'e' sh oo
th ee
gh
st

ALPHABET CHART

EXPLAINED

If your child has trouble with spelling words, or dyslexia or difficulty "tracking" as they read, here are some tips that will help you help them. I have had many school teachers very receptive to allowing your child have a lamented chart on his or her desk.

Color code each letter of the alphabet as you see on the alphabet chart. Make the chart and keep it in a place where the child can see it often, such as the refrigerator or bathroom wall. The letters "b," and "d,", "B" and "D" are in red. Those letters are red to make them stand out from the rest of the letters on the chart. Children with reading difficulties sometimes flip "b" and "d" or "B" and "D" around, or mistake them for each other. One of the first signs of a child having difficulty in reading is that they flip these two letters around or mistake them for each other. Being the only two letters in red, they always stand out from the rest of the letters. Learning to correctly recognize "b," "d," "B" and "D" is a huge accomplishment!

Remember that spark I told you about? This is a good one!

- Make a special "pointer" to point to each letter as you say the letters with your child. (IS THIS WHAT YOU ARE TRYING TO SAY?)
- Make letters out of different colors of Play Dough or homemade modeling clay. This is so important for a child that needs tactile learning or has dyslexia. Here is a simple recipe for making your own modeling clay. Add food coloring to each batch and keep in separate freezer zip lock bags.
- Adding a little hand lotion of any kind to dough that is drying out, will soften and moisten the dough!!

Basic Modeling clay ingredients ratios:

2 cups flour

2 cups warm water

1 cup salt

2 tablespoons vegetable oil

1 tablespoon cream of tartar (optional for improved elasticity)

- Make words using the different-colored playdough clay letters.

- Ask your child to make "three purple letters," "one red letter," etc.

- Help your child write their school spelling words in the Sparkle Colors. Write each letter in the color that is on their letter chart. If you write each word on a 3x5 card, it makes for easy spelling practice and review.

- Make cards for each letter. (out of paper, 3 x 5 cards, cardboard, etc. get creative) You can play the letter 'matching game', spell words, sound out each letter, etc. and so on, using letter tiles.

- At the grocery store: let your child hold a letter card. Ask your the child to find that letter as you walk down the aisles. Point out the letter, if that letter is in the item that you put into your grocery cart. When they find the letter, it goes into a "I DID IT" baggie and you give them the next letter.

- Keep a baggie of the letter cards in the your car. Standard 3x5 cards are great for this. Look for letters on billboards as you drive. Also, keep a baggie of letter cards on the your kitchen table.

- Play the letter matching game with the spelling words, play hide and seek with the spelling words, and make up a silly story with the spelling words.

- REWARD! REWARD! REWARD! Think of creative ways to reward your child. Each letter they find at the grocery store can add up to earn them points, be an extra minute of TV time or staying up past bedtime, etc.

EMOTIONAL INSTRUCTION

Use the Sparkle Emotion Page instructions to start dialog between you and your child, use words from this list.

Make it a game. There are several options here. Do not lead your child to an answer. Tell them that there is no wrong answer. Whatever color they assign to that emotion is correct for them in this moment.

The following is one game idea, feel free to make it your own:

Match a Sparkle color to an emotion. Remember, there is no right or wrong. If your child places the emotion of embarrassment in ORANGE, deep inside maybe they may have been were embarrassed because they felt or thought that someone had made a bad decision. If they place it in RED, maybe perhaps they felt powerless or too fearful to move. If they place it in BLUE, maybe they may have been too afraid or nervous to say something to change the situation before they became embarrassed. Etc.

Match the correct Sparkle color to a healing word. To help heal the harmful emotions, find an opposite word from a word on the list. For example, teach your child to replace "anger" with "calm." GREEN is for calmness. You do not have to go into depth in a deep explanation. You could can simply say, "A way to feel better when we are angry is to use our GREEN for calmness."

Draw a picture of the emotion word, using only Sparkle colors.

IDENTIFY YOUR EMOTION

A TIME WHEN I FELT........

Happy _____

Sad _____

Love _____

Frustrated _____

Accepted _____

Rejected _____

Joyful _____

Lonely _____

Supported _____

Embarrassed _____

Excited _____

Ashamed _____

Proud _____

Humiliated _____

Confident _____

Overwhelmed _____

Secure _____

Insecure _____

Silly _____

Shy _____

Surprised _____

Jealous _____

Hopeful _____

Remorse _____

Brave _____

Afraid _____

Scared _____

Angry/mad _____

QUICK TIPS

FOR USING THE SPARKLES IN ME IN YOUR CHILD'S LIFE

- Make flash cards of the Sparkles colors, and where they are on the body.
- Have your child wear solid-color clothing. This is a huge help! Let your child pick what color they want to wear and pay attention to your child's color choices. It will provide insight into what they are dealing with on a deeper emotional level.
- Socks! Love, love, love solid-color socks! You can suggest a color of socks for your child to put on when you see the need for a certain Sparkle color. For example, a YELLOW pair of socks will help your child have more confidence while taking that spelling test at school. A simple, "These yellow socks are great! And they show off your YELLOW Sparkle for that test today!"
- Color in a blank gingerbread man.
- Food coloring is king! Put food coloring in milk, water, mac and cheese, etc. Use this as

encouragement and as a reward. For example, with GREEN say, "I think you could use a little GREEN so you will be kinder to your sister, so let's put a drop of green into your milk." Or, "I am so proud of you for sharing that I made you green mac and cheese!"

- Organize toys by color.
- Use solid-color cubbies.
- Bracelets! Make them out of yarn or other materials. Wearing a Sparkle color bracelet is an excellent reminder of what Sparkle color your child is working with. For instance, a BLUE bracelet can help them tell the truth.
- At bedtime, set up a Sparkle dream with your child, and ask what they dreamed about the next morning. The dreams always have four things: a mode of transportation, something to wear, a companion, and your child is always the hero. For example, if you are setting up a RED Sparkle dream, your child may pick a fire truck, a red cape, a red dog. In the morning you ask them to tell you about their dream. Ask about the fire truck, the people in the dream, their cape, what their dog looked like, and who they saved or what they did as the hero.

- Make a matching game. Match the color of the Sparkle to the power words, Bible verses, where they are on the body, foods, and so forth.
- Play hide and seek. Hide toys, flash cards and other items, and as your child finds them, ask them to tell you things about that Sparkle color.
- Look for Sparkle colors as you are riding in a car. Instead of saying the color, say the key color words from The Sparkles In Me poem. For example, "Let's find something that is a WISE color," and then look for something that is orange.
- Rewards, rewards, rewards!!!! Give them stickers of the Sparkle colors. Rewards go a long way with children.
- Make up your own silly Sparkle songs.

VISUALIZING

THE SPARKLES IN ME COLORS

Children have such great imaginations! They can easily see things in their mind's eye. I think sometimes as adults we forget that, and simply do not use it to our child's advantage. I encourage you to help your child see the Sparkles in themselves.

Ask questions. Describe what yours are to you. Ask them to describe what their Sparkle colors look like to them. Maybe they see the Sparkles as balls of lights, or fireworks. One of my sons saw his Sparkles as glowing balls "like the moon," while the other saw them as bursting fireworks.

Try not to lead your child into seeing what you want them to see. Be patient. (It is fascinating to me that after a child learns The Sparkles In Me sometimes they will tell me that their Sparkles have changed.) As a parent who just wanted her child to have peace, I know how frustrating it can be when your child says, "I don't see anything."

Take heart. They see it. They feel it. They just may not be able to describe it out loud. That's okay. There is no wrong answer in The Sparkles In Me. There is only progress. You want the best for your child and you want it right now! But, give it time. The conversations will come.

STORIES

FOR EACH COLOR

In this next section, you'll find fun stories to accompany each color. These stories will help to better display each color and the meaning behind it.

Go through each story for each color as a way of familiarizing your child with the significance of each color. This is a fun and easy way to engage your child's imagination and to cause them to recognize the emotion behind each color. They are great conversation starters!

THE LION CUB

A RED SPARKLE STORY

A mother lion and her cub were walking through the African grassland. They were on their way to the river to get a drink of water. The young cub asked his mother, "Mom, why is every other animal in the jungle afraid of us? When I try to run and play with the giraffes or zebras, or even the elephants, they all look at me, some bow, and then they all walk away!"

The Lioness smiled and proudly put her shoulders back. She held her head up high and answered her cub, "The other animals know who you are. They know who you belong too. They know your family. They know who your father is. They know your father is the King of the land. This makes you very special."

The lion cub did not like this answer. Being special and a child of the King did not sound like such a good thing if it meant other animals would not want to play games or splash in the river together.

The lion cub thought maybe it was not a good or fun thing to belong to the lion family. So when the lion cub and lion mother reached the river, the cub had an idea. He thought to himself, "Maybe if I go off by myself and am not seen with any other lions, the other animals will not recognize me, and then they will play with me."

While his mother was getting a drink of water and talking with the other lion mothers, the lion cub snuck off to play downstream, away from the lion family. This was very dangerous. Not all animals who came to drink from the river were nice. Some were very sneaky and mean. And some would like nothing better than to attack and eat a young lion cub. Some were crocodiles.

The young lion cub walked farther and farther away from the lion family. He splashed and splashed in the water and looked for other animals to play and splash with. He was so busy trying not to be recognized as a lion that he did not see how far he had walked away from the other lions. He also did not see the old crocodile who sat across the river on the riverbank watching him. And he most definitely did not see when the old crocodile slithered down into the water and started slowly swimming toward him.

When the crocodile was closer to the lion cub, he raised his head slightly above the water and asked, "What are you doing there? Are you all alone? Splashing around in that water sure looks like fun!"

The young lion cub did not want to be recognized. He thought if this crocodile didn't know he was a lion, then they could play and splash in the river together. So, he answered, "Oh, hello! I am – uh, I am just a little friendly animal playing in the river, nobody special or anything. Would you like to splash around in the water and play with me, too?"

The old crocodile smiled and replied, "Of course. That sounds like great fun. I will swim closer to you and make big splashes for you."

So the old crocodile began to swim even closer to the young lion cub. But all of a sudden the old crocodile stopped and raised his head up clear out of the water!

"Come on and play!" said the young lion club as he splashed and splashed in the water.

The old crocodile got a scared look on his face and he began swimming backwards away from the young lion cub. "Oh no!" said the old crocodile, "Why didn't you tell me who you really are?! If I come any closer to you, your father will attack and destroy and kill me. I must quickly get back to the other side of the river!"

As the old crocodile raced to get away in the river, the young lion cub heard a strong low, deep breath behind him. He turned to see his father, the mighty Lion, the King of all the land, standing behind him on the river bank.

The father lion told his son, "That old crocodile was not your friend. He was trying to trick you. If he had gotten any closer to you he would have dragged you under the water and killed you."

The young lion cub did not understand why the old crocodile retreated in such a hurry. "Father, why did the old crocodile swim away in such a hurry and act so frightened? You did not run into the water to attack him."

The father lion stood with his shoulders back and held his head up high. He told his son, "I did not have to run into the water to attack that old crocodile, son. All I had to do was stand still and let him see me. The old crocodile was afraid because he knows who I am. He knows who you really are. He knows he cannot harm you without me finding out about it, and he does not want to challenge me to a fight. He knows he would not win."

"As for you my young lion cub, you must remember who you really are. You are a child of the King. You are set apart from the other animals. You are special. All of the other animals look up to us and know that as long as I stand on the river bank, all can come and drink water in peace."

As the young lion cub followed his father back to the his mother, he pulled his shoulders back, walked proudly and head his head up high. He remembered who he really was. He was a child of the King.

BERNARD THE BULL
A RED SPARKLE STORY

Mertle the Farmer was hoppin' mad! "All right! That's it! I have had enough! If that bull gets out of that gate one more time and tramples my garden I am gonna THWACK him on his nose with my garden rake! I have told him over and over to stay out of the garden, but he just doesn't listen!"

Bernard the Bull got into trouble on the farm a LOT. He just couldn't help it. He got out of his gate a lot. It wasn't *his* fault if the gate would easily open if he bumped it just right. It wasn't *his* fault if the chickens would flap their wings and act all crazy when he ran through the barn yard. It wasn't *his* fault if he had to go through Mertle's garden to be close to her. He just couldn't help himself.

And why did Bernard the Bull love to be close to Mertle the Farmer? Because she had the most wonderful singing voice, and she sang sweet little songs while she worked in her garden. All of the animals loved Mertle the Farmer. But Bernard loved her most of all.

Early one morning Bernard heard Mertle singing. "She must be in the garden!" he thought to himself. "Hooray! Mertle, here I come!" He got so excited. He bumped the gate just right and it flew open. He ran through the barnyard as fast as he could go. But, he didn't really watch where he was going.

He didn't realize that he knocked over the horse's water bucket. He didn't realize that he ran right through where the chickens were eating some grain, making them flap their wings and scaring them half to death. Chickens squawked and threw their feathers everywhere! All Bernard the Bull was thinking about was Mertle's beautiful singing voice, and he was headed straight for her garden!

When Mertle the Farmer heard the chickens going crazy, she knew what was coming. A very large bull named Bernard was coming – coming right for her garden! Mertle stopped singing and said, "Okay, Bernard, today I am ready for you. I hate to have to do this, but you have to learn to stay out of my garden!" She jammed her garden rake down into the ground and pulled the long handle way back. Then she waited. And here came Bernard, running right into her garden and running right up to her!

As soon as Bernard was close enough, Mertle let go of the garden rake handle and it sprang forward. THWACK! The handle hit Bernard the Bull right on his nose! It hit him so hard that it knocked him on his rear end! He just sat there thinking he saw little stars swirling around his head.

"I'm sorry boy, but I warned you," said Mertle the Farmer. Then she led Bernard the Bull back to his field and closed his the gate.

But what do you think happened the next morning? The next morning when Bernard heard Mertle singing again, he bumped his gate just right and it flew open. He just knew Mertle was working in her garden. So, he started running through the barnyard towards Mertle and her beautiful singing voice!

But he didn't pay any attention where he was going. So it wasn't *his* fault when the horse's water bucket got knocked over and splashed water all over the horse's face. And it wasn't *his* fault that he accidentally, lightly, kicked a chicken and the chicken got so scared that it fainted. Silly chickens.

When Mertle looked up from raking and saw Bernard the Bull headed right for her garden and for her, what do you think she did? She jammed her garden rake into the ground, and pulled the long handle back and waited.

When Bernard the Bull got close enough, THWACK! The rake handle hit him on the nose and down he went. There he sat, with a hurting nose and seeing little stars swirl around his head.

Mertle the Farmer was a bit upset at Bernard the Bull. "Just look what you have done to my garden!" she shouted. When he looked all around at Mertle's garden, Bernard got very sad and embarrassed. He felt so bad. He had not realized that he had torn up her garden.

He certainly had not *meant* to tear up her garden. But there it was. Smashed lettuce, mangled green beans, and smooshed flowers lay all over the ground.

Mertle just couldn't figure it out. Why did Bernard keep opening his gate and trampling her garden? But when she put Bernard back into his field she heard a songbird singing a little song. Then she saw Bernard's ears perk up and he turned his head like he was looking for the songbird! Could that be it? Bernard liked her singing!!
"That's it! He is coming to hear me sing!" she said. "Well, I think I have a good solution that will make the whole barnyard happy."

That night Mertle was very busy hammering and sawing. She was making something. The next morning, Bernard waited and listened, but he didn't hear Mertle singing.

He went to his gate and saw Mertle the Farmer coming to him with a rope. She opened his gate and put the rope around his neck. Slowly she led Bernard the Bull all the way through the barnyard.

The horse whinnied and swished her tail as Bernard walked by. The chickens still went crazy, squawking and throwing feathers, and one of them still fainted. Silly chickens.

Mertle the Farmer led Bernard the Bull to his new pen, which was right beside her garden. She told him, "I am so sorry that I didn't understand you were just trying to be close to me because you like my singing."

Bernard gave Mertle a great big lick across her whole face. That was to say, "I am sorry I tore up your garden, and tell the horse and the chickens I am sorry too."

Mertle the Farmer shut the gate of Bernard's new pen. "Now, don't bump this one open. I promise I will be right here, fixing my garden...and singing."

Bernard the Bull gave Mertle the Farmer one more great big lick across her whole face. That was to say, "Thank you."

And the whole barnyard – even the crazy chickens – lived happily ever after.

BIG RED

A RED SPARKLE STORY

Once there was a super hero named Big Red. He was big and strong and all the people in the town counted on him to protect and look out for them. Whenever there was a fire, Big Red came in his big red fire truck and put the fire out. At the intersections of the streets Big Red put big red stop signs, so trucks and cars would stop and not run into each other. At the end of a sunny day Big Red would fly up to the sunset and paint beautiful shades of red in the sky.

But the most interesting thing about Big Red were the red boots and the red cape he wore. One day a little boy asked Big Red , "Why do you wear big red boots and a big red cape?"

Big red answered, "I wear my big red boots to remind myself and everyone else that every step I take is important. When there is danger, I must be quick to go to help. I must be strong and powerful so I can help rescue someone in danger and protect them from harm. Red is a color people notice right away and they pay attention when they see it. The big red cape helps me to fly into the sunset. I paint beautiful shades of red into the sunset to remind everyone that they also have strength and power. When you see red in the sunset remember your own strength and power. I wear the red cape so everyone can easily see me. The red cape stands out. Not everyone wears a red cape you know."

If you were a super hero what would your super hero look like? What would you have or wear that would stand out and help you be quick to help others?

WISE GRANDFATHER OWL WITH ORANGE EYES

AN ORANGE SPARKLE STORY

"Get it! Get it!"

"It ran over that way! You get it!"

The two big farm cats popped their heads out of the field.

"Which way did it go now?" asked the first big farm cat.

"It went that way! Over there! Get it! Get it!" shouted the second big farm cat.

And away they went. The two big farm cats took off running this way and that. They were chasing a big, fat, juicy rat. Because, cats eat rats, you know.

Now, Up above all of this running around business, sitting quietly in a tree, was a little young owlet and his Wise Old Grandfather Owl with big orange eyes. The moon was shining bright in the night sky, and the little young owlet was hungry for breakfast. Because, owls wake up at night time, you know.

The little young owlet stretched his feathery wings, yawned and asked, "What's going on down there, Grandfather? It is awfully noisy."

"Oh, those two big farm cats are chasing a big, fat, juicy rat through the field," replied his Wise Old Grandfather Owl with big orange eyes.

The little young owlet got very excited. "Oh, goodie, goodie! Let's go chase it, too! I sure am awful hungry!" He started hopping up and down on the tree branch and flapping his wings. Because, owls eats rats too, you know.

"Shhhh," whispered Wise Old Grandfather Owl with big orange eyes. "Not yet. Wait. Be still. Watch. Listen."

"Ah-hah! I think I got him!" Up popped the first big farm cat out of the weeds, then down he went again. "Shucks! I missed him!"

The second big farm cat yelled, "I see him! I see him! He went that way! Get him!" Up popped the first big farm cat again, "What?! Where?!"

"Over there! Over there!" shouted the second big farm cat. And they were off running again, this way and that, chasing a big, fat, juicy farm rat. Because cats, eat rats, you know.

"Grandfather, I see the big, fat, juicy rat!" said the little young owlet. "Let's swoop down and get him. He sure would make a fine breakfast!" Because owls eat rats, you know.

"Shhhh," whispered Wise Old Grandfather Owl with big orange eyes. "Not yet. Wait. Be still. Watch. Listen."

Well, this went on for a very long time, thought the little young owlet. Those two big farm cats running and running all over the field, chasing a big, fat, juicy rat. The little young owlet just wanted to swoop down and get the big, juicy rat himself

But his Wise Old Grandfather Owl with big orange eyes kept telling him, "Shhhh. Not yet. Wait. Be still. Be watching. Be listening." And all that shushing, waiting, and being still, and watching, and listening was getting pretty boring.

It looked like the two big farm cats were having all the fun. And the little owlet had to stay on his tree branch, and be shushed, and be still, and be watching, and be listening.

"But why can't I fly down there and catch the big, fat, juicy rat right now?" asked the little young owlet.

His Wise Old Grandfather Owl with big orange eyes answered, "If you fly down there now, while those two big farm cats are running all over the field, they might catch YOU instead. Because big farm cats will eat little owlets too, you know. So, for now, shhh. Not yet. Wait. Be still. Watch. Listen."

Soon the big farm cats began to get tired. They got so tired of running and not catching the big, fat, juicy rat, that they stopped running, and fell fast asleep instead.

The Wise Old Grandfather Owl with big orange eyes stood and stretched out wide his big, feathery wings. "Now," he said.

The little young owlet stood and stretched his feathery wings too. "Now what?" he asked. Wise Old Grandfather Owl with big orange eyes said, "Now. Tell me, what do you see?"

"I see the two big farm cats fast asleep," answered the little young owlet.

"Now, tell me what do you hear?" asked the Wise Old Grandfather Owl with big orange eyes.

The little young owlet leaned his ear toward the field. "I hear the two big farm cats snoring!"

Wise Old Grandfather Owl looked into the field with his big orange eyes, "Ahh, you are right. And guess who else has grown so tired and has fallen asleep? A big, fat, juicy rat.

"Now, little owlet. You were patient. You watched. You listened. You waited. And now, the big farm cats are asleep and the danger has passed. Now you can swoop down and easily catch the big, fat, juicy rat with your claws, and we will have a yummy, yummy breakfast!"

Because owls eat rats too, you know.

FATIMA THE ROYAL ELEPHANT

AN ORANGE SPARKLE STORY

Once upon a time in a faraway land, there lived a young Royal Princess and her favorite Royal Elephant, named Fatima (Fa-teem-a). The Royal Princess and Fatima were together every day.

The Royal Princess's favorite color was orange. So, if she ate an orange, Fatima also ate an orange. When she got her fingernails and toenails painted, a beautiful orange color, of course, Fatima also got all of her toenails painted a beautiful orange color.

For every parade, the King would tell the Royal Elephant Caretaker, "Choose the best and finest Royal Elephant to carry the Royal Princess in the parade today." Fatima was always the elephant chosen. All of the elephants knew this. And all the elephants remembered.

For the parades, the Royal Princess would wear a beautiful orange dress. She wore a beautiful orange veil on her head. She wore strings of gold and orange jewels around her neck. She wore orange and gold rings on her fingers. She wore gold bracelets on her wrists. Her fingernails and toenails were painted a beautiful orange color. Gold ribbons were wrapped up in her hair.

Fatima would also be dressed for the parades. A shiny, beautiful, orange blanket was draped across her big, strong back. Beautiful orange veils were placed across her strong, wide forehead. Long strings of gold and orange jewels were put around her strong neck. Gold ribbons were wrapped around her long, beautiful tusks. Gold bracelets were put on her strong legs. All of her toenails were painted a beautiful orange color. Together, the Royal Princess and Fatima were a beautiful sight to see when they were in the parades!

When they passed by all the people in the town who had lined the street, the people would bow to the Royal Princess. When Fatima passed by all the other elephants that lived in the town, the elephants would make loud noises with their trunks, and they would bow their heads low to the ground. The elephants knew who Fatima was. The elephants remembered.

One day a horrible, scary, strong storm came to the town. It rained and rained and rained. The rain did not stop for many days. It rained so much that the river next to the town overflowed its banks and flooded the whole town. The flood knocked down many buildings and trees.

The people in the town were so scared that they all ran to higher ground for safety. Except one. The Royal Princess had been caught up in the rushing river waters and was quickly swept away.

All of the elephants also ran to higher ground for safety. Except one. Fatima jumped into the rushing river waters and went after the Royal Princess to save her. But soon they were both lost in the rushing river waters.

After the storm and after the flood waters had gone away, the King sadly announced to the people in the town that the Royal Princess had been lost in the rushing river waters. They all thought she was gone forever and they were all very sad. The King had a sad walking parade to remember the Royal Princess.

But the King did not make an announcement about Fatima. None of the people in the town thought to remember Fatima. They did not have a sad walking parade for her. But the elephants knew what Fatima had done. The elephants bowed their heads low to the ground. The elephants remembered.

THE SPARKLES IN ME

Many days past passed. The people of the town began cleaning up the knocked down buildings. The elephants helped pick up the knocked down trees. Suddenly, the elephants began to make loud noises with their trunks! All of the people in the town rushed to the street to see what was going on. It was Fatima! She was walking to the Royal Palace and she was carrying the Royal Princess on her back! Fatima had saved the Royal Princess from the rushing river waters and they were coming home!

All of the people cheered! They were so happy to see their Royal Princess return safe and sound. But no one thought about the elephant carrying the Royal Princess. The people did not cheer for Fatima for saving the Royal Princess. But the elephants bowed their heads low to the ground as Fatima passed by them. The elephants knew. The elephants remembered.

The King was so happy to see his daughter that he threw a very big party for all the people in the town! But the King forgot about Fatima, the Royal Elephant who had saved his daughter from the rushing river waters. Fatima did not go to the party. She wasn't even taken in to the Royal Elephant yard to get fine food. This broke Fatima's heart. She did not like being separated from her best friend, the young Royal Princess.

Fatima was so sad that she left the town. She went to live in the wilderness all by herself. All alone. The people of the town soon forgot all about Fatima. But the elephants would bow their heads low to the ground. The elephants knew. The elephants remembered.

Years went past. The Royal Princess grew up. And now was the day that she would become the Queen. A big, fancy parade was planned in celebration. The King told the Royal Elephant Caretaker, "Choose the best and finest Royal Elephant to carry the Royal Princess in the big and fancy parade today. And from now on, that Royal Elephant will have only the best and finest food, and will have the best place in the Royal Elephant yard, and be well taken care of the rest of its life!"

So, when it was time for the parade to start, all of the people in the town lined each side of the street. They were so excited to see their Royal Princess become their Queen! The King stood in front of the Royal palace at the end of the street, and waited to see his daughter in the big, fancy parade. He knew she would be riding on the best and finest Royal Elephant!

The parade started. The King waited to hear the shouts and cheers from all the people in the town, but the shouts and cheers did not come. He waited to hear all of the elephants make loud noises with their trunks, but the loud noises did not come. He looked way down the street. Then he saw what was happening.

All of The people stood quiet, and all of the elephants had their heads bowed low to the ground. The King did not understand this. Then he saw his daughter riding an elephant, coming down the street toward the Royal Palace. She was so beautiful. She wore a beautiful orange dress. Her fingernails and toenails were painted a beautiful orange color. She wore a beautiful orange veil on her head. She had long strings of gold and orange jewels around her neck. She wore gold and orange rings on her fingers and gold bracelets on her wrists. She wore gold ribbons wrapped up in her hair.

Then the King saw the elephant the Royal Princess was riding on and he was not happy! The elephant was old and walked so slow. It looked tired and weary. Its skin was wrinkly and there were scars on its body. And the elephant had been dressed in Royal parade dressings! The King was not happy to see his beautiful royal Princess riding on the back of this broken down, wrinkly, old elephant!

The elephant had a shiny, orange blanket draped across its skinny back. The blanket was all crooked. An orange veil drooped across the elephant's wrinkly forehead. The veil hung so low and uneven that it was covering one of the elephant's eyes. Long strings of orange and gold jewels weighed down the elephant's wrinkly neck. Big gold bracelets clanked loosely on the elephant's wrinkly and skinny legs. Gold ribbons hung from the elephant's broken tusks.

The King yelled at the Royal Elephant Caretaker, "What have you done?! I told you to choose the best and finest Royal Elephant to carry the Royal Princess today! This elephant is old and weak! Just look at it! None of the orange and gold Royal parade dressings fit it properly! Its body is scarred and its tusks are broken! What have you done?! This is NOT such an elephant the Royal Princess should be riding on in the big and fancy parade today!"

The Royal Elephant Caretaker smiled as he looked at the elephant, who was carefully and slowly carrying the Royal Princess towards them. Then he turned to the King and said, "Oh, King, but I did choose the perfect Royal Elephant to carry the Royal Princess today.

That elephant is Fatima, the Royal Elephant who saved the Royal Princess so many years ago. When she was not remembered or taken into the Royal Elephant yard, she went away.

She has been living alone in the wilderness for all of these years. When you told me to choose the perfect Royal Elephant for the big and fancy parade today, and that elephant would be well taken care of for the rest of its life. The Royal Princess asked me to go into the wilderness, and find Fatima, and bring her home."

Well, now the King was embarrassed and sorrowful. And he felt ashamed. He walked up to Fatima and put his hand on the side of her tired, old face.

"Oh, my dear Fatima. Please forgive me. It was you who saved our Royal Princess all those years ago, and I had forgotten all about you. How could I have forgotten such a brave and fine Royal Elephant? From now on you will have the best place in the Royal Elephant yard and you will have the finest of food and care. And as a sign of your bravery and friendship with the Royal Princess, your toenails will always be painted a beautiful orange color!"

Then Fatima put her tired old trunk on the King's shoulder, as a sign of forgiveness. All of the people of the town cheered. All of the elephants in the town made loud noises with their trunks, then they bowed their heads low to the ground. The elephants had known who Fatima was all along. The elephants remembered.

BELLY BUTTON BUNNY

AN ORANGE SPARKLE STORY

Once there was a bunny named Belly Button. She won the spelling bee at her school. The prize was a juicy big orange! Belly Button bunny was so excited! That was a very good thing that happened.

But at lunch time, Belly Button Bunny dropped her tray of food, and her prize orange rolled all the way across the floor. The school kids laughed at her. That was a very bad thing that happened.

At recess Belly Button helped a little girl bunny climb onto the monkey bars so she could play. The little girl bunny said, "Thank you , Belly Button. You are very kind!" That was a very good thing that happened.

On the way home from school, as Belly Button walked down the side walk, a car raced by and splashed in a big mud puddle. The mud splashed onto Belly Button, and got her dress and her back pack all muddy and dirty. Belly button cried, because she loved her dress and her back pack.. That was a very bad thing that happened.

Then Belly button heard a little robin bird yelling, "Help! Help Please someone help me!" Belly Button ran down the side walk. She saw the little robin bird. Some big mean birds were poking their beaks at the little robin bird and picking on him. Belly Button ran up to the big mean birds and thumped them hard with her back feet. Bunnies have very strong back feet. Belly Button thumped those big mean birds so hard and they went flying up in the air and flew away. "Oh, Thank you Belly Button. You are very brave," said the little robin bird. That was a good thing that happened.

Then Belly Button picked up her back pack and started down the side walk to home. She didn't see the hole that was in her back back, and as she was walking, some of her school books fell out onto the ground and she lost them. That was a bad thing that happened.

Then Belly Button saw a little puppy about to run into the road to get a ball she was chasing. "Stop!" yelled Belly Button. "You can't just run into the road without looking for cars!" So Belly Button made the little puppy stay on the sidewalk. Then Belly Button looked both ways and made sure no cars were coming. She walked into the road and got the ball for the little puppy. "Oh, thank you, Belly Button! You are very wise to look both ways for cars before you walked into the road to get the ball for me." That was a good thing that happened.

When Belly button got home, she stopped on the front porch and took off her back pack. She was so excited to show her mom the prize orange she had. Then Belly Button noticed the hole in her back pack and the some of her school books were missing. AND, there was mud all over the prize orange. Belly Button was so upset that she just sat and cried, "So many bad things have happened today! I just don't know what to do!" Then Belly Button's mom came outside and sat down next to her.

Belly Button told her mom all about the bad things that had happened that day at school and on the way home. Her mom told her she would talk to her teacher about the missing school books. Then she said, "Belly Button, while you were walking home today from school. I got a few phone calls. And the phone calls were about you. Let me show you something special."

Then Belly Button's mom took the orange and held it in her hands. "You are like this orange," she said. "It is a prize, and special just like you are. The really real good stuff is on the inside of the orange. You have to peel away the bad tasting skin on the outside to get to the really real good stuff inside." Belly Button's mom then took the orange and peeled away a little bit of the skin, "This is like you dropping your tray at school. We will just peel away that bad thing and not think about it anymore."

As Belly Button's mom peeled away the orange skin, they talked about the bad things that had happened that day. One by one, Belly Button's mom took pieces of the yucky outside skin and threw it away. And the bad things that had happened that day were forgotten about.

"Now look Belly Button," said her mom. "This is the really real good stuff inside the orange. Just like your really real good stuff is inside of you. Your teacher called me and said that you helped a little bunny girl today at recess. She said you are very kind. Mrs. Robin called and said you protected her little robin bird from some mean big birds. She said you are very brave. Mrs. Dog called and said that you stopped her little puppy from running into the road. She said you are very wise to look both ways for cars when you got the ball for her little puppy.

Then Belly Button's mom broke open the orange. "See" she said, "The really real good stuff is inside the orange and it is good fruit to eat." She held up a piece, handed it to Belly Button, and said, "Belly Button, you are kind." She handed Belly Button another piece and said, "Belly Button you are brave." She handed Belly Button bunny another piece and said, "Belly Button, you are wise." Then she kissed Belly Button bunny on the forehead and said, "Belly Button, just like this prize orange, you have lots, and lots, and lots of good really real good stuff inside of you and I am so happy that you are my little bunny."

WOLFY WOLFINGTIN WOLFENSPOON

A YELLOW SPARKLE STORY

The little wolf pup sang, "I am Wolfy Wolfingtin Wolfenspoon, and I howl at the Big Yellow Moon!" He sang it over and over and over. He was practicing for the moment when he would announce his name to the whole wolf pack. It was a very big deal.

Once a year all of the new wolf pups stood in the middle of the wolf pack circle. There they told the whole wolf pack the name he or she had chosen for themselves. This would be the name they would be known as from now on. And the name had to be chosen very, very carefully. It was a very big deal.

Hunter Wolf came over to Wolfy Wolfingtin Wolfenspoon and asked him, in a not so nice way, "What on earth are you doing?!"

"I am practicing my name song for the Big Yellow Moon ceremony tonight," answered Wolfy Wolfingtin Wolfenspoon.

"You can't do that. You can't sing a name song," said Hunter Wolf, in a not so nice way.

"Why not?" asked Wolfy Wolfingtin Wolfenspoon.
Hunter Wolf smirked and said, in a not so nice way, "Because no one has ever done that before, that's why."

"Well, that is the name in my heart and that is the name I am choosing." So Wolfy Wolfingtin Wolfenspoon found another place in the woods to practice singing his name song. He was very proud to be a wolf and he was thankful for the Big Yellow Moon who that lit up the night sky. It was a very big deal. He sang, "I am Wolfy Wolfingtin Wolfenspoon and I howl at the Big Yellow Moon!"

Soon another wolf heard him singing and came over to him. It was Speedy Little Wolf. She had chosen that name because she was very small, and she was a very fast at running. "What is that noise?" she asked, in a nice, shy way.

"Oh, it's me!" said Wolfy Wolfingtin Wolfenspoon. "I am practicing my name song for the Big Yellow Moon ceremony tonight."

Speedy Little Wolf shook her head and said, in a nice, shy way, "It's kind of different. I am not sure you can to do that. You might want to choose something else to call yourself."

"But that is the name in my heart and that is the name I am choosing," said Wolfy Wolfingtin Wolfenspoon.

"Okaaaay," said Speedy Little Wolf, in a nice, shy way, "But I don't think you should do that. No one has ever sang a name song before."

So Wolfy Wolfingtin Wolfenspoon found another part of the woods to practice singing his name song. He was very proud to be a wolf and was thankful for the Big Yellow Moon that lit the sky at night. He sang, "I am Wolfy Wolfingtin Wolfenspoon and I howl at the Big Yellow Moon!" It was a very big deal.

His best friend, Fisher Wolf, heard him singing and came up to him. Fisher Wolf asked, in a best friend kind of way, "Well, you aren't really going to choose that long, weird name are you? What if you stand in the middle of the circle and sing that weird name song and everyone laughs at you?!'"

"Well, you have a weird name," answered Wolfy Wolfingtin Wolfenspoon.

"Well, my dad told me to pick that name because I am really good at catching fish right out of the river with just my mouth. But I didn't put it into a song!"

"Well, it is the name in my heart and the name I am choosing," said Wolfy Wolfingtin Wolfenspoon.

"Well, okaaaay" said Fisher Wolf, in a best friend kind of way. "I will see you tonight at the ceremony."

The sun set. The Big Yellow Moon was high in the sky. All of the wolves gathered around into a big circle. When it was Wolfy Wolfingtin Wolfenspoon's turn to step into the middle of the circle, he walked into it proudly and cleared his throat. Then he sang his name song.

"I am Wolfy Wolfingtin Wolfenspoon and I howl at the Big Yellow Moon!"

After he finished singing his name song, the silence from all of the other wolves was a very loud silent. Hunter Wolf smirked. Speedy Little Wolf shook her head. Fisher Wolf hid his eyes with his paws. Then, all of a sudden, the leader of the wolf pack walked into the middle of the circle and spoke to Wolfy Wolfingtin Wolfenspoon.

"My son, why have you chosen this unusual name, and why did you choose to put it into a song? No other wolf has ever done that before."

Wolfy Wolfingtin Wolfenspoon looked up at the wolf leader and said, "You see Sir, it is because I am very proud to be a wolf and I am very thankful for the Big Yellow Moon that lights up our way at night."

The leader of the wolf pack thought and thought for a long time. All of the other wolves still remained silent, but it was a very loud silent. Then the leader of the wolf pack spoke to Wolfy Wolfingtin Wolfenspoon again. "My son, you have chosen your name very thoughtfully." Then he announced to the whole wolf pack, "From now on this little wolf pup will be known as Wolfy Wolfingtin Wolfenspoon, because he is proud to be a wolf and he is thankful for the Big Yellow Moon that lights up our sky at night. Let us all learn his name song so we can always be reminded of how good it is to be a wolf and that we should always be thankful for the Big Yellow Moon. Wolfy

Wolfingtin Wolfenspoon, will you sing your name song again for all of us?"

"Yes Sir!" said Wolfy Wolfingtin Wolfenspoon proudly. "I am Wolfy Wolfingtin Wolfenspoon and I howl at the Big Yellow Moon!"

It was a very big deal.

THE GREAT BANANA TREE

A YELLOW SPARKLE STORY

It was morning in the jungle. Today was Marcello's big day. Today was the day Marcello would make his parents proud. Today he was going to climb the Great Banana Tree. Today Marcello would get his own banana all by himself! Marcello was a monkey.

His grandfather and father had made the climb up to the top of the Great Banana Tree when they were his age. All of his older brothers had made the climb, too. Now, today was Marcello's big day. And all of the monkey troop would be watching.

"I am so nervous Mother!" said Marcello. "What if I fall, or if I can't make it all the way up to the top of the Great Banana tree? It's the biggest and tallest tree in the whole jungle!"

Marcello's mother licked her palm and then slicked down a piece of unruly fur on top of his head. "Have you been doing your swinging and climbing exercises like you were supposed to?" she asked.

"Yes, ma'am," replied Marcello.

"And have you listened to all of your father's instructions about climbing and how to pick the best banana from the bunch, when you get to the top of the Great Banana Tree?" his mother asked.

"Oh, yes, ma'am! Every word!" said Marcello.

His mother put her hands on his Marcello's shoulders, looked him in the eyes, and told him, "Then you will be fine. Remember what you have learned. This day is what you have been training and working so hard for. Now go to your father. He is waiting for you."

As Marcello walked toward the Great Banana Tree, he was so scared that his legs felt wobbly, his head was spinning, and his heart was pounding! Every monkey in his jungle was there to see him pass his final climbing test.

If he could climb all the way up to the top of the Great Banana Tree and get his own banana, then Marcello would be allowed to climb on his own from now on! He wouldn't have to stay with his mother and all the other monkey mothers and their little monkey kids when he climbed. If he passed this test, he would become a man in his family!

There standing underneath the Great Banana Tree was Marcello's father. He was a big and brave monkey. Marcello admired him very much.

Marcello's father told him, "I am climbing to the top of the Great Banana Tree, Marcello. I will wait for you there, son. When you join me at the top of the Great Banana Tree, we will share a banana together!"

And then his father climbed up the Great Banana Tree and was soon so high he was out of sight. It was a very, very, very long way to the top!

Marcello took a deep breath. "Ok, here I go!" he said. And he started to climb and climb and climb. He used his hands and his feet. He remembered his training and climbed with his best moves.

"I can do this," he told himself. The climb was much harder than he thought it was going to be, but he kept climbing. Every once in a while his father would yell down, "Marcelllllooooooo! Keep coming! You can do it. I believe in you!"

And Marcello would yell to the top of the tree. "I am here, Father! I am still climbing! I can do it!"

A couple of times, Marcello missed a branch he was jumping or reaching out to and he fell back a few branches. But, he kept climbing. It hurt when he fell, but he kept climbing. A couple of times, Marcello looked down and saw how very high he had already climbed. That scared him!

He was already so high up off the ground. He had already climbed very, very high, but he wasn't yet to the top of the Great Banana Tree. It was taking longer than Marcello thought it would. But, he kept climbing.

"Marcelllllooooooo! Keep coming. You can do it! I believe in you!" the little monkey would hear from somewhere high above him. And Marcello he would answer back, "I am here, father! I am still climbing! I can do it!"

When Marcello reached the very top of the Great Banana Tree, he saw his father's big and strong hand reach down and pull him up to sit on the highest branch with him. Marcello looked around and could hardly believe what he saw! He could see the whole jungle from the top of the

Great Banana Tree! It was so beautiful! It made Marcello happy to be a monkey.

"Well done my son!" said his father. "You climbed all the way to the top of the Great Banana Tree all by yourself. From now on you will be able to climb in the trees whenever you wish, and not have to stay with the mothers and little monkeys. Now, pick the best banana you see from the bunch and we will eat it together."

So Marcello picked the biggest, yellowest, greatest banana he could find. At the top of the Great Banana Tree, as the sun was setting in the jungle, sat two monkeys, sharing a banana and being happy to be monkeys.

DANDELION'S BRIGHT IDEA

A YELLOW SPARKLE STORY

Two little dandelions had been asleep underground all winter long. Now it was time to wake up. Daniel Dandelion yawned. He felt some heat from up above him and wondered where it was coming from. His sister Darcie Dandelion was waking up, too. She shivered in the cold, dark dirt. "Brrrr, it is cold," she said.

"I have a bright idea!" said Daniel Dandelion. "Let's reach up and find out where that heat is coming from."

"I don't know," replied Darcie Dandelion. "We have never been up there before. We don't know what is up there. It could be scary. Let's just stay here." Daniel Dandelion looked at his sister and said, "It will be okay. You have to try."

So she did.

Two little dandelions pushed up, up, up through the

ground. Daniel Dandelion said, "I can barely see a bright yellow light. That must be where the heat is coming from. I have a bright idea! Let's keep reaching up just a little farther and break through the ground. Then we'll find out what that bright yellow light is." "I don't know" replied Darcie Dandelion. "We have never been above the ground before. And I am already so tired from trying to push up through the ground. Let's just stay here."

Daniel Dandelion told his sister, "It will be okay. Come on. You have to keep trying."

So she did.

Two little dandelions reached up and broke through the ground. The heat felt wonderful. They turned their little dandelion faces towards the bright yellow light. The light was so bright they had to squint their eyes.

"What is that?!" exclaimed Darcie Dandelion.
"I think it is called the sun," replied Daniel Dandelion.

"It's hot!" said Darcie Dandelion.
"It sure is!" said Daniel Dandelion. "Isn't it wonderful? I heard that this bright yellow sun will help us grow. I have a bright idea! Let's open our eyes very slowly and get used

to the light. Then we can look around and see where we are."

"I don't know," said Darcie Dandelion. "We have never been above ground before. We have never lived in front of the sun before. How do we know it will help us grow?" Daniel Dandelion told his sister, "Come on. Open your eyes. You have to have faith. You have to try."

So she did.

Two little dandelions opened their eyes. They stretched out their stems and leaves. They got used to the sunlight and they really liked it! Daniel Dandelion looked around and saw that they were in a beautiful grassy field and that field was full of other dandelions who had also pushed up through the ground.

"I have a bright idea!" he said. "Let's stay here and grow and blossom into our bright yellow flowers and enjoy the bright yellow sunshine!"

This time Darcie Dandelion smiled and opened her eyes up wide. She decided she could grow in the beautiful green grassy field and enjoy the warm sunshine, too.

So she did.

THE LITTLE BOY'S REALLY REAL SELF

A GREEN SPARKLE STORY

An old man and a little boy sat together on a bench in a beautiful and special park.

"I'm not happy," said the little boy.

"Oh?" asked the old man. "Why not?"

"I just don't feel like my really, real self today. Maybe I should be a different myself," answered the little boy.

Just then the little boy saw a cheetah running past them. "Wow!" he exclaimed. "Look at that! I think I wanna be that!"

So the little boy turned himself into a cheetah. And off he ran. He did what the other cheetahs did. He was the fastest cheetah in the park. He won all the cheetah racing games.

Soon the other cheetahs didn't want to play with him anymore because he always won and they always lost. He became very lonely. So he turned himself back into a little boy and went back to the bench, and sat with the old man.

"I'm still not happy," whined the little boy.
"You didn't like being a fast cheetah?" asked the old man.

"No. It wasn't my really, real self and it got very lonely," replied the little boy.

Then the little boy spotted a beautiful big bird flying high up in the air. "It must be wonderful to fly! I want to be that!" shouted the little boy.

So the little boy he turned himself into a big beautiful bird and flew way, way, way up into the air. He thought that was very fun. He did what the other birds did. He built a nest. He chirped and sang along with the other birds. But when it became supper time, and he saw the birds eating worms, he had a change of heart. So he changed himself back into a little boy and went back to the bench, and sat with the old man.

"You didn't like being a big beautiful bird?" asked the old man.

"No," replied the boy. "It wasn't my really, real self. They eat worms! Who does that?! That's just gross."

The little boy sighed. "But I am still not happy. I just don't feel like my really, real self."

Then the little boy saw a fish jump up out of the river. "Wow! That looks like fun! I want to be that!" shouted the boy.

So the little boy ran and jumped into the river and turned himself into a fish. He swam and swam and swam. He jumped up out of the water and made big splash landings. He did what the other fish did. But pretty soon he got bored. It turned out that mostly the fish just swam around. They didn't play or even talk to each other. Being a fish was not for him. So he hopped up onto the river bank, turned himself back into a little boy, and went back and sat on the bench with the old man.

"So, you didn't like being a splashy fish?" asked the old man.

"Not at all," replied the little boy. "Fish don't run, or play, or even talk to each other. But, I am still not happy. I don't feel like I am my really, real self."

Then the old man showed the little boy a picture of his dog. "This is my best friend," he said. "He is loyal to me. I can count on him. We play fetch and we talk together. He makes me happy every day. I miss him. I love him very, very much. I am sitting here waiting for him to come back to me, so we can go home."

"Where did he go?" asked the little boy.

"Well, he didn't feel like he was himself today. He wasn't very happy. I think he just forget how important he is just being his really, real self. So, he went exploring, I guess. He said he wanted to be something else. He said he wanted to be a different himself. I told him I would stay here on the bench and wait for him until he was ready to go back home."

The little boy scooted up next to the old man and said, "Well, I didn't like being a cheetah, or a bird, or a fish. It didn't make me happy. I bet I would be happy just being your dog."

"That would make me very happy, too," said the old man. "I love that dog very, very much."

"I love you, too," said the little boy. "And I will be happy being my really, real self, and I am ready to go home now."

And with that said, the little boy turned himself back into a happy, little dog...who was his really, real self. Then the little boy and the old man went home together.

THE LITTLE TURTLE

A GREEN SPARKLE STORY

"Oh, it's just a stupid turtle," said Macon, as he rode up closer to the little, green lump in the road.

Macon and Ralphie were speeding down the country road on their bicycles. They were going to town to buy some candy and pop with their allowance money. "Move, you stupid turtle. You are on my side of the road!!" Macon shouted.

"Maybe we should stop and help it across the road," suggested Ralphie.

"No way," said Macon. "The store closes in ten minutes. If we don't hurry we won't get there in time. Besides, that turtle shouldn't be in the road in the first place! Why isn't it over in the grass where it belongs, anyway?"

So the boys rode on. Ralphie looked back and saw the little turtle slowly making its way across the country road. "I sure hope it makes it across the road alright," he thought to himself. But he kept riding his bicycle, hurrying to get to the store.

Ever so slowly, the little turtle kept walking across the country road. She was going as fast as she could, step, step, step, step, but everyone knows turtles are not very fast. Little Turtle prayed, "Oh, please God, please don't let any cars come and hurt me. Surely I could not get out of the way of an oncoming car in time."

By the time Little Turtle was halfway across the road, she was so tired. It was a long way across the road for a little turtle. She did not think she could go one step farther. But she knew she could not stop to rest.

Then, Little Turtle heard a noise. A terrible noise, A horribly, frightening noise. It was a dangerous roar off in the distance. "What is that?!" thought Little Turtle. "Where is that noise coming from?!" Little Turtle began to be very afraid.

The dangerous, roaring sound got louder and louder. "Maybe it is a bear who is coming to eat me up!" thought Little Turtle. But she soon learned that is wasn't a wild animal at all. The dangerous, roaring sound was the sound of horses and their riders Susan and Brenda coming down the country road.

Susan yelled to Brenda, "Come on slow poke! Can't your horse go any faster?!"

Susan laughed and tapped the stirrups into the side of the horse to make it go faster. She wasn't thinking about where she was going. She had ridden her horse down this road many times. She also wasn't thinking something could be in the road, either. But this time, there was: Little Turtle.

When Little Turtle saw the horses galloping toward her she became so frightened that all she could do was pull herself into her shell. This is what turtles do when they do not feel safe. So there lay Little Turtle, all tucked up into her shell, lying in the middle of the country road.

"Look out!" shouted Brenda. "Susan, look out! There's a turtle in the road!"

But it was too late. Susan's horse kicked Little Turtle with one of its hooves as it ran by her. Little Turtle spun around and around and finally flipped over onto her back. And there she lay – on her back – in the middle of the country road.

The two girls kept riding. Brenda said, "Maybe we should

go back and check on the little turtle. At least we should move it out of the road."

Susan shook her head and waved her friend on. "No. It's okay. That little turtle was probably already dead, anyway. I mean, it was just lying there in the middle of the road."

After the horses were gone, Little Turtle stretched out her head and her legs. She knew she was in much, much trouble. Not only was Little Turtle on her back, but her shell had a small crack in it. Now, it is not a good thing for a little turtle to be stuck and stranded on her back. If she could not get herself flipped over soon, she would die. She would lie there, and die. If the crack in her shell was too severe, she would die.

She wiggled and wiggled, and stretched this way and that, for a long, long time. But it was no use. Little Turtle could not get flipped back over and onto her feet by herself. She was so scared and struggling so much to right herself that she didn't hear a car coming. And here Little Turtle was, lying upside down in the middle of a country road!

But this was no ordinary car. The car slowed down when the driver saw Little Turtle in the road. The car stopped – right there in the middle of the road! Then a wonderful thing happening. A very kind and wonderful thing happened. The man driving the car turned on blue lights that were on top of the car. It was a policeman in his police car.

The policeman got out of his police car and came over to Little Turtle, who was still struggling to get herself flipped over onto her feet. "There, there little one," said the policeman. "Let me help you."

He gently reached down and cupped Little Turtle in his hands. He walked to the side of the road and sat her down on her feet. When he sat Little Turtle down on the ground he saw that her shell had a small crack in it. "Oh, my" he said. "Well, I can't just let you loose now. It looks like you really need some help."

The policeman took Little Turtle to a nearby veterinarian. He told the veterinarian, "Please take good care of the little turtle. I am sure she is pretty shook up and hurt. Do whatever you have to do to make her well. I will come back in a few days and pay the bill."

A few days later, the policeman went back to check on Little Turtle. The veterinarian told him, "I have fixed the wound as much as I can. And I had started this little turtle on medication so she won't get an infection, but I am

THE SPARKLES IN ME

afraid she would never survive again in the wild. Her shell will never be as strong as it was before she got hurt."

The policeman smiled and said, "Oh, that is just fine. I will pay the bill and take the little turtle home with me. I have a big beautiful farm she can live on and I will take good care of her."

Little Turtle was so happy. "How kind this man is," she thought to herself.

On the way home, the policeman reached down and petted Little Turtle softly on her back. He looked down at her and told her, "Everything is going to be just fine. Don't you worry." And he wasn't sure, but he thought he saw Little Turtle smile back up at him as if to say, "Thank you, sir. You are a very good and kind man."

RUNS-SO-FAST

A GREEN SPARKLE STORY

Once there was a little boy. An Indian boy. A Lakota Indian boy. His name was Runs-So-Fast. He got that name because he was always in a hurry. He ran everywhere he went. Everywhere!

If his mother told him to go to the river and bring back some water, Runs-So-Fast would run to the river. He would get the water alright. He would dip a large gourd that was made just for holding water into the river and fill it up full. But as Runs-So-Fast would run back to his mother's lodge, most of the water would spill out onto the ground. "Oh, I forgot. I'm sorry," Runs-So-Fast would say.

If he went hunting with his father, Runs-So-Fast would often get carried away and he would run up on ahead. This was not a good thing to do on a hunt. This would spook whatever animal they were hunting. This meant no food would be found on that hunt. "Oh, I forgot. I'm sorry," Runs-So-Fast would say.

If he played racing games with the other children, he would always win, of course. And, Runs-So-Fast was the best messenger in his village, of course. He could deliver a message from one person to another, from one side of the village to the other, faster than anyone else.

But sometimes Runs-So-Fast would be so excited about running all the way through the village that he would not remember the whole message he was supposed to deliver. "Oh, I forgot. I'm sorry," Runs-So-Fast would say.
But one bright and sunny day, Runs-So-Fast saw his life change in a big way.

On this day, Runs-So-Fast was sent to go look for signs of the big buffalo herd. It was time for his people to move their village and follow the buffalo across the land. His people needed the buffalo for food and clothing. Runs-So-Fast was very proud and happy to be chosen for this great honor.

"I was chosen because everyone knows how fast I can run!" Runs-So-Fast said. "I will run so fast until I can see clues of where the buffalos have gone. Then I will run back as fast as I can and tell my people. Everyone will be so proud of me!"

Runs-So-Fast took in a deep, long breath, then he took off running as fast as he could go. He knew he must run very far if he was to be able to see or hear any clues as to where the big buffalo herd may be grazing in the vast prairie. He ran and ran and ran.

When he had come to a tall, steep, grassy hill, he heard a small, soft voice. "Hello. Hello up there. Where are you going in such a hurry? Please stop. I must tell you something important!"

Runs-So-Fast stopped in his tracks! He looked all around him. He did not see a person or a bird or an animal. He shrugged his shoulders and said, "Humph. I must be hearing things in my imagination." So he took off running again. He made it half way up the tall, steep, grassy hill. Then he heard the small, soft voice again.

"Hello up there. Please stop running. Please stop! I must tell you something important." Again, Runs-So-Fast stopped running and looked all around. He saw nothing. This time, Runs-So-Fast decided to answer the small, soft voice.

"Who's there? Where are you? I can't see you."

"Down here," said the voice. Runs-So-Fast looked down at the ground, but he did not see anything.

"Where? Where are you?" he asked again. The small, soft voice replied, "I am down here beneath your feet. I am the Grass. And I can help you find the buffalo."

This excited Runs-So-Fast very much. "You can? Where are they? How far do I have to run to find them? How can you help me? You are just grass." The Grass said, "If you will stop running long enough, and be still and calm, I can help you. Lie down on the ground and be very still."

Runs-So-Fast did as the Grass instructed him to. He lay down on the ground with his face looking up toward the sky. He felt kind of silly. Shouldn't he be running up the great big hill to find the buffalo?

Not wanting to be rude, because Indian children are taught to respect all of nature, Runs-So- Fast politely said, "Excuse me, but I don't see how you can help me find the buffalo. You are just the grass here on the hill side."

"Ahh," said the Grass. "But I am not only here on the great hillside. I am all over the whole land. And because of that, I can see very much, I can hear very much and I can feel very much. Much more than you can.

"I can see the birds fly across the sky, and the sun, and the moon and the stars long before you can see them in your village.

I can feel the wind coming to your village way before you know it is coming. And, I can hear and feel the big herd of buffalo as they move on the ground. If you will be calm and still I can teach you these things also."

Runs-So-Fast was very happy to hear this. "Oh yes!" he said to the Grass. "Please teach me. I will listen and learn."

The Grass told Runs-So-Fast to look up at a nearby tree. "Do you see the leaves moving?"

"Yes, I do," answered Runs-So-Fast.

The Grass said, "That is how you know the Wind is blowing. Now close your eyes".

Runs-So-Fast did as he was told. The Grass asked him. "Do you feel the Wind on your face? Do you feel which direction the Wind is coming from?"

"Yes I can," answered Runs-So-Fast. The Grass said, "Make your heart and mind very calm. Slow down your breathing. Feel yourself lying on the ground. Now, can you smell what the Wind is carrying to your nose?"

Runs-So-Fast did as he was told. Very soon he smiled and said, "Yes! I can smell the buffalo!"

The Grass said, "Now put your ear to the ground and make your heart and mind very calm. Slow down your breathing. Tell me Indian boy, can you hear what is walking upon the Grass far away?"

Runs-So-Fast whispered, "Yes. I hear them. I can hear the buffalos. Many, many buffalos walking upon the Grass."

The Grass waved in the wind, very pleased with Runs-So-Fast. "The Wind has told you that the buffalos are coming. The Grass has told you how far away they are. If you would not have stopped to listen, you would have run a far way, and in the wrong direction! Well done Runs-So-Fast.

"Now go back to your village and tell your people to get ready. Tell your people that you have found the buffalos and they are coming."

Runs-So-Fast thanked the Grass for its wisdom and kindness. Then he ran as fast as he could back to his village to tell them the good news.

BIG MAMMA BLUE BEAR'S CROOKED AND WIGGLY PINKY TOE

A BLUE SPARKLE STORY

It was the time of the year when the river was full of big salmon fish. There were so many big salmon fish that all a little bear cub had to do was stick their head into the water, chomp down, and they would come up with a big salmon fish in their mouth!

And Big Mamma Blue bear had her group of little bear cubs ready to go get those fish! She was called Big Mamma Blue because her black fur was so black, that in the sunlight sometimes it would shine a little blue color, but that is another story.

She knew getting to the river was a little tricky. A young bear cub could easily get lost in the big forest if they didn't know the way to get to the river.

So every year, Big Mamma Blue bear gathered up the new cubs to show them how to get to the river, so they could chomp down on some big salmon fish. She made it a game!

"Gather around little cubs," said Big Mamma Blue bear. "Oh! It's going to be so exciting! Today is the day you'll find your way to the river and chomp down on the big salmon fish! Yum, yum!"

Little Missy bear cub raised her paw and asked, "You mean you aren't just going to take us there, like follow the leader?"

"No hunny bear," replied Big Mamma Blue. "We aren't going to play follow the leader. I will be waiting for you at the river. You are going to have a scavenger hunt. There are clues all along the way from here in the middle of the big forest to the river. You just have to look for them. Now, everyone grab a back pack and be on your way."

But Little Missy bear cub was nervous. What if she looked and looked, but couldn't find any clues?! What if she didn't find her way to the river? And if she did make it to the river, what if she didn't catch a big salmon fish? Oh, how much she just wanted to be a little, little bear cub again, and her mom would just bring her food to eat. That was so much easier.

Theodore bear cub grabbed his back pack, tagged Little Missy bear cub on the shoulder as he ran past her, and shouted, "Come on slowpoke! I'll race you to the river!"

As the other bear cubs got their back packs and ran after Theodore bear cub, Big Mamma Blue bear yelled out, "Remember to look for the clues! Pay attention to where you are walking!"

Little Missy sighed, "Okay feet. Let's get going, I guess."

Big Mamma Blue bear patted her on the head and told her, "You'll be fine. Just pay attention to where you are walking. I will see you when you get to the river."

"But what if I get lost in the big forest?" asked Little Missy bear cub.

"If you really get lost, I will come and find you." And with that, Big Mamma Blue bear disappeared into the big forest with one big bear leap.

Little Missy bear cub took one step. Then she remembered what Big Mamma Blue bear had said: "Pay attention to where you are walking." She looked down at the ground and saw Big Mamma Blue's big paw print. She stepped into that paw print. Her own little paw was soooooo tiny compared to Big Mamma Blue's paw print. She could see where Big Mamma Blue's claws had sunk deep into the ground. All except for one claw, that is. The pinky toe claw print seemed to be a little crooked and wiggly. "That's funny," thought Little Missy bear cub. "Big Mamma Blue has a crooked and wiggly pinky toe."

Little Missy bear cub put on her back pack and headed into the big forest to look for clues and find her way to the river so she could chomp down on some big salmon fish. Just thinking about those fish made her belly growl with hunger. Up ahead she heard Theodore bear cub holler, "Hey! I found something! I think it's a clue! I am going to put it in my back pack!"

Little Missy bear cub ran towards the voices of the other bear cubs and found all of them looking at a bird feather. "Oh cool!" said one bear cub.

"That's really neat! You are so lucky!" said another.

"Yeah," said Theodore bear cub. "It must be a clue because birds fly to the river to get water to drink!" He put the bird feather in his back pack, then scampered off into the big forest, with the rest of the bear cubs following him.

Except for Little Missy bear cub. She looked down at the ground and noticed another big bear paw print that had a crooked and wiggly pinky toe. "Big Mamma Blue must have come this way," she thought to herself. "But I didn't see her come this way and none of the other bear cubs said they had seen her, either. But that is definitely her paw print. I would know that paw print anywhere."

She looked all around and there was another big bear paw print just like that one! So she took a few more steps and saw yet another big bear paw print with a crooked and wiggly pinky toe. "Big Mamma Blue must have come this way!" she said out loud. So she decided to follow those paw prints, even though it was in the opposite direction from where all the other bear cubs had gone. Even though she thought it was the right way to go to find the river and the big salmon fish, she was still a little scared. Soon, she couldn't even hear the other bear cubs' voices in the big forest anymore.

She kept walking. She wasn't finding anything she thought would be good clues to show her the way to the river, but what do you think she did keep finding? Big bear paw prints with a crooked and wiggly pinky toe! All day long Little Missy bear cub found her way through the big forest, looking for clues. She hopped over logs, scooted under bushes, and even tried to climb some big rock piles. She found broken twigs that she thought were strange looking. She found some bird feathers like Theodore bear cub had found, and she even found an old turtle shell. But nothing felt like it was a good clue. At least not a good enough clue to put in her back pack. As interesting as those things were, she didn't think they would help her find the river and the big salmon fish.

Meanwhile, in a different part of the big forest, the other bear cubs were finding all kinds of things and putting them into their back packs. Everything they saw that they thought was interesting they were putting into their back packs! Twigs, feathers, old snake skins, rocks, animal bones, leaves – everything that a little bear cub might find interesting, went into their back packs. And those back packs were soon full and very heavy to carry. But do you think all of those interesting things would help them find their way to the river and the big salmon fish?

When the sun was starting to go down in the sky, Little Missy bear cub heard a wonderful sound. A wonderful, watery sound. A wonderful, watery, fish splashy sound! She stood up on her hind legs and looked out around her. There it was! The river and the big salmon fish! And standing in the middle of the river chomping down on a big salmon fish was Big Mamma Blue bear!

"I found you! I found the river and the big salmon fish, too!" cried out Little Missy bear cub. "Look at all those big salmon fish!" She ran to the river, stuck her head in the water and chomped down on a big salmon fish. She popped her head up out of the water with the fish still in her mouth and said, "This is fantastic!" Then she plopped down on the river bank and began to eat her fish.

Big Mamma Blue bear said to Little Missy. "Great job! I knew you could do it! But where are all the other bear cubs?'

"I don't know," answered Little Missy bear cub, still eating her big salmon fish. "I didn't go the same way they did. And if they aren't here, then they must be lost in the big forest."

"Hmmm," said Big Mamma Blue bear. "It will be dark soon. I must go and find them. The big forest at dark time is no place for little bear cubs to be all alone."

So Big Mamma Blue and Little Missy walked through the big forest in search of the lost little bear cubs. It didn't take her long to find the little bear cubs, because Big Mamma

Blue knew every inch of the big forest and she was very good at following little bear paw prints and finding little lost bear cubs.

When Big Mamma Blue and Little Missy found the lost bear cubs, they were all sitting together with their back packs. They were scared, and tired, and hungry. "Oh, Big Mamma Blue, are we happy to see you!" exclaimed Theodore bear cub. "We looked for clues all day, and our back packs are full of stuff, but we still didn't find the river." The little bear cubs dumped out their back packs full of rocks, sticks, feathers, old snake skins, and other interesting stuff.

Theodore asked Little Missy, "Did Big Mamma Blue find you too?" "Nope," said Little Missy bear cub proudly. "I found the river. Annnnd I ate a big salmon fish!" "Really?!" asked Theodore. "What clues did you find? What's in your back pack?"

Little Missy bear cub held her back pack upside down and shook it. Nothing fell out of it.

"But it's empty! You didn't find any clues at all," said one of the bear cubs.

Big Mamma Blue bear patted Little Missy on the head and told the other bear cubs, "Little Missy *did* find some clues.

Those clues were right in front of all of you all the time, you just didn't see them. Maybe you just didn't think they were clues."

Then Big Mamma Blue stomped her foot into the ground, making her big bear paw print. "Little Missy saw my paw prints and followed them all the way to the river. Little Missy, how did you know they were *my* paw prints and not some other bear's paw prints?"

"Oh, that was easy," said Little Missy bear cub. "When you were first talking to us in the middle of the big forest, you left a paw print there. Your paw print has a crooked and wiggly pinky toe. So when I saw more paw prints like that, I just kept looking for them and followed them, and then I found you and the river and those yummy fish!"

Theodore bear cub asked Big Mamma Blue bear, "But how did *you* know how to get to the river all by yourself with no paw prints to follow?"

"Well," replied Big Mamma Blue, "When I was a little bear cub, my Big Mamma bear showed me how to follow her paw prints all the way through the big forest to the river. And I knew my own Big Mamma's paw prints very well and what they looked like. I knew those paw prints anywhere! So I have been to the river many, many times before. I know the way."

Little Missy looked at Big Mamma Blue's foot that had the crooked and wiggly pinky toe and asked her, "Big Mamma Blue, how come your pinky toe is all crooked and wiggly?"

"Ohhhh!" laughed Big Mamma Blue. "That happened the very first time I found the river. I was so excited! I jumped into the water with a big splash! I guess I scared a big salmon fish, because it bit me right on my pinky toe leaving it all crooked and wiggly!" Then she lifted up her big foot and shook it, wiggling her crooked and wiggly pinky toe. All the bears laughed and laughed.

And as the bear cubs walked back to the river with Big Mamma Blue bear to chomp down on some big salmon fish, they would lift up their paws and shake them, and act like they had a crooked and wiggly pinky toe, too.

SIR TERRANCE AND THE STRANGE BIRD

A BLUE SPARKLE STORY

There was a horrible Beast roaming the village and the lands. Some said it was like a fiery dragon, that it lived in a mountain cave and would swoop down onto the village and burn up the crops. No one in the village was smart enough to know when the horrible beast would come.

Some said it was like a huge hairy Beast who was so strong it would knock over whole trees to block roads, so the villagers couldn't chase it when it grabbed up the sheep with its huge claws and ran off with them. No one in the village was strong enough to move the fallen trees.

Some even said it was a hideous monster Who's scary snarls and eerie sounds were so scary to listen to that when the villagers heard them, they would run into their houses and hide. Then the scary monster would just walk all around the village stealing whatever it wanted. No one was brave enough to confront the horrible beast.

The villagers knew there was only one person who could defeat the horrible Beast. Sir Terrance the Smart and Brave and Strong. Surely he could kill the Beast and save the village. So Sir Terrance started on his journey to defeat and kill the Beast.

As he was climbing up the mountain to the mountain cave, a strange looking bird flew down from the sky and landed above him. The bird had stubby and hairy feathers. It's beak wasn't smooth like other birds, but it was all bumpy and clicked together when it talked. It's legs were long and fat and it's claws were black and sharp. It's eyes were so red that they looked like glowing fire.

"Who are you and what are you doing here?!" screeched the strange bird.

Still climbing, Sir Terrance answered, "I am Sir Terrance the Smart and Brave and Strong and I am hunting a horrible Beast who is attacking the village."

"Hmmm," mused the strange bird. "And what will you do if you find this beast?"

"I will kill it, of course."

"You?!" laughed the strange bird. "Just you?!"

"Me, and my mighty sword," answered Sir Terrance.

This annoyed the strange bird very much, so it scratched some rocks loose from the mountain with its black sharp claws.. It blew a wicked breath and blew the rocks down the mountain.

The rocks fell all around Sir Terrance, knocking his sword loose. The sword fell down the mountain to the ground. Without his mighty sword, Sir Terrance knew he could not defeat the Beast. So, Sir Terrance had no choice but to climb back down the mountain to retrieve it.

"Haw-haw-haw!" shrieked the strange bird. You are not even smart enough to climb this mountain and hang onto your "mighty" sword. You're dumb. You will never catch the Beast!" And as the strange bird flew away it yelled, "The beast is not in the mountain cave! The Beast is tooooo smart for youuuuu!"

Sir Terrance retrieved his sword and started to walk into the forest where some said the beast lived. As he was walking in the forest he began to hear big crashing sounds and feel little shakes deep in the ground.
All of a sudden the strange bird was there, walking alongside him.

"What are you doing here?!", screeched the strange bird.
"I am hunting a horrible Beast who is attacking the village" replied Sir Terrance.
"And what are you going to do if you find this "beast?" asked the strange bird.

"As I told you before, I am going to kill it."

"Hmmm" mused the strange bird. Then the strange bird leaned up against a large tree and began to use it to scratch his back and laughed, "You sure don't look strong enough to kill this beast all by yourself."

Sir Terrance replied, "I have my mighty sword that will do the killing for me."

Then a huge tree came crashing down right in front of Sir Terrance! It fell with such a quick and loud thud that Sir Terrance barely had time to jump out of the way! When the tree hit the ground, the ground shook so hard that it knocked the sword out of his hand and had blocked the road Sir Terrance was on. He had no choice but to find his sword and find another way out of the forest.

As he was walking out of the forest Sir Terrance saw the strange bird flying away and squawking, "The beast isn't in the forest. You will never catch the beast. You are not strong enough to move even one fallen tree! You are weak! The beast is tooooo strong for youuuuu!"

Sir Terrance headed toward the village. When he was just inside the village that strange bird again appeared by his side.

"What in the world are you doing here?!" screeched the strange bird.

"As I told you before, I am hunting a horrible Beast who is attacking the village", replied Sir Terrance.

"Hmmm" growled the strange bird. "And what will you do if you fine this beast."

"With my mighty sword, I will kill it" said Sir Terrance.

Soon Sir Terrance began to hear scary snarls and eerie sounds. The strange bird was nowhere to be seen. All of the villagers were so scared that they ran into their houses and hid. "Please save us! Save us!" cried the villagers. "Find this horrible beast and destroy it!"

Sir Terrance looked up into the sky and saw the strange bird flying away. As it flew away it cackled, " The beast is not in the village! You will never catch the beast! You are not brave enough to hear scary and eerie sounds! You are scared! The beast is tooooo scary for youuuuu!"

Three days later, Sir Terrance was sitting on the shore of the lake, near the village. He was sharpening his mighty sword. And who do you think came strolling up along the shore, dragging it's sharp, black claws?

The strange bird ruffled its stubby and hairy feathers, and clicked its bumpy beak together. Sir Terrance did not look up at the strange bird, but kept sharpening his mighty sword. "You are right bird" he said. "The Beast was not in the mountain cave, or in the forest, or in the village."

"Hmmm, you don't say" gloated the strange bird. "I told you that you were not going to catch the beast you were hunting. You are not smart enough, or strong enough or brave enough. You are dumb and weak and scared. You will never catch that beast and it will go on destroying villages forever."

Sir Terrance stopped sharpening his sword, looked at the strange bird and said, "Oh, but I believe I have caught the horrible Beast and it stands here before me."

The strange bird gulped – hard. "Who me?! Surely not. Why I am just a silly little bird. I could never do those horrible things that the beast does."

In a flash Sir Terrance jumped to his feet and held out his mighty sword to the strange bird. Written on the blade sword were the words KNOWLEDGE – BRAVERY- STRENGTH. And written on the handle of the sword was the word TRUTH.

When the strange bird saw the written words on the sword and saw his reflection in the shiny sword it knew it was caught. The bird watched as his reflection in the sword turned into a fiery dragon, then into a huge hairy beast, and then into a scary monster and the back into the strange bird.

Sir Terrance said, "I have known all along that you are the beast. I only had to let you think you had bullied me and stopped me, so I could lure you out here to the water's edge. Now with my mighty sword I will kill you and throw your body to the bottom of the lake forever."

And he did. With one mighty strike of the sword, the horrible Beast was gone, thrown into the bottom of the lake forever. And the Villagers and Sir Terrance lived happily ever after.

MOLLY THE WHALE

A BLUE SPARKLE STORY

It was summer time. Molly and her big family were on vacation. They were all swimming in the Mediterranean Sea, on their way to Egypt. Near Egypt the fish were big and there were lots of them. So every year Molly's family swam there on their summer vacation to get their bellies full of fish. Molly and her family were whales.

Molly loved to swim with her cousins. They loved to play tag and chase each other through the deep, deep water. Sometimes though, they would have to be reminded of the rules. Molly's father would say, "Now remember kids, stay close to the rest of the grownups. Do not swim out too far ahead all by yourselves. And when you go up for air, get in a good deep breath and dive down deep again. Do not stay near the surface too long. There are dangers up there that you do not understand."

Molly the Whale was a good little whale, most of the time. Most of the time she obeyed her parents. But, Molly had two big problems. And these big problems got her into to trouble A LOT!

Problem ONE was sometimes Molly wanted to do just what she wanted to do and not listen to her parents. Problem TWO was Molly would not always tell the truth, especially when she was caught doing just what she wanted to do instead of minding her parents.

Yep, these were big problems. And one day these big problems put Molly and her mother in great danger.

While Molly and her cousins were swimming and playing chase, Molly saw something way up ahead, dangling in the water. "Hey look guys! What is that?" Molly said, "I have never seen fish fins like THAT before! Let's go check it out!" One of her cousins said, "You know we aren't supposed to swim too far ahead all alone. We could get lost or something."

"Yeah" said another one of her cousin. "Our parents said we are supposed to stay close to them."

"Humph," replied Molly. "Well, I want to see what that dangly thing is. Come on, we will just swim over there real fast and be back before our parents even know we are gone! It will be fun!"

But Molly's cousins shook their heads and said, "Nope. We all need to stay swimming along where our family is swimming. We need to listen to our parents. There must be a reason they don't want us to swim too far ahead all by ourselves."

"Okay, you big chickens!" mocked Molly. "Well, I am going all by myself then! I want to see what that dangly thing is, and I will be the only brave one to swim out there and get it!" And off she went swimming away from her family as fast as she could swim. Farther and farther away from her family, Molly swam out ahead, alone, in the big sea.

When Molly got to the dangly thing, she couldn't believe her eyes! It was something she had never seen before! It was the weirdest looking fish she had ever seen! It had two long skinny things swishing back and forth in the water. It had two shorter skinny things splashing around on top of the water. It had two eyes right on the front of its big head, and scrunchy, brown seaweed on its head. And it was making some loud awful noises.

Molly was so excited! "My cousins won't believe it! I have got to show them this weird dangly fish! They will think I am really cool when I come back and show it to them!"

So Molly opened up her great big whale mouth. She swam faster and faster, right up to the weird dangly fish in the water, and scooped it up right into her mouth! Molly thought she was pretty cool for doing just what she wanted to do.

But then something happened that Molly did not plan on happening. While she was racing back to her cousins, she accidentally swallowed it! She had swallowed the weird dangly fish! And right away she started to feel really, really sick to her stomach.

"Well, what was it?" asked one of Molly's cousins. "Oh, it was nothing," Molly said. "Uh, it was just a shadow of a big bird flying over the water or something. There wasn't really anything dangling in the water at all."

This was a big problem.

As Molly and her whale family swam along, Molly's stomach felt sicker and sicker. "What's the matter dear?" asked her mother.

"Oh, nothing," answered Molly.

"You don't look so good," said her father. "You haven't been swimming out too far ahead along have you? You didn't eat anything that we whales don't usually eat, did you?"

"Oh no, Father! I would never do that. Not me," said Molly.

This was a big problem.

Well, Molly just got sicker and sicker. But she didn't want to tell her parents that she had accidentally swallowed the weird dangly fish. She did not want to admit that she had disobeyed, swam out way too far all by herself, and she had been showing off. And she really did not want to get caught telling lies and not telling all of the truth. That was a big problem.

"It will be okay," Molly told herself. "I did just what I wanted to do anyway and I had fun. Besides, I was the only one brave enough to swim way up ahead all by myself! Now my cousins will be jealous of me because I am very cool!"

But it wasn't okay. After a little while, just by looking at Molly, her parents knew she had been up to something. They knew Molly looked very sick to her stomach.

The big whale family was almost to Egypt when Molly swam up to her mother. "Mom, I don't feel so good. I think I am going to be sick!"

"Oh dear!" replied her mother. "Let's quickly get you closer to the shore line so you can rest a little in the shallow waters."

So Molly's mother told the rest of the family to swim on ahead and that her and Molly would have to catch up.

Molly's mother was NOT happy. "Alright Molly, swim over here close to the beach with me and rest a little while. I hope the family does not get too far ahead of us. It is very dangerous for whales to swim all alone. When we are all together we are safer from the whale hunters. After you feel better, we will have to swim fast and in the deep water to catch up to them and stay safe."

"Yes ma'am," said Molly sadly. Her stomach was doing flip flops and she did not feel good at all. But she still did not want to admit that she had swallowed the dangly fish. Now she and her mother were stuck here, away from the rest of the family. She still did not want to tell the truth.

That was a big problem.

"Molly," said her mother, "are you SURE you didn't swim up ahead and do anything else you weren't supposed to do? Did you eat anything us whales are not supposed to eat?"

Molly shook her head, which made her stomach feel even more flip floppy.

"Oh, no I didn't Mom. I am sure."

That was a big problem.

Annnnd then it happened. Right then and there Molly felt it coming. She could feel the dangly fish in her stomach and then in her throat, and then ....BLAAHHHGGGEEHHH! Molly threw up all over the beach! And out came the dangly fish!

"Molly Jellyfish Whale!" her mother yelled. Uh-oh, mom had used Molly's whole name! She was really mad! "What did you do?! You swallowed a whale hunter?! We do not eat whale hunters! No wonder you were sick to your stomach! So you DID swim up ahead all alone and you lied about it. And you lied about eating a whale hunter! You are in big trouble Missy! Just wait until I tell your father!"

Molly looked over to the dangly fish she had just thrown up onto the beach. It just sat there shaking its head all gooey and slimy. But that is another story.

Molly's stomach now felt better, but her heart didn't. She had lied to her parents and now she had put herself and her mother far away from the safety of her family. This as a big problem.

"Well, come on Molly," said her mother. "We will have to swim fast to catch up with our family. Then your father and I will discuss your punishment."

But just as Molly and her mother had started to swim back out into the deep sea, Molly saw her father swimming toward them. He had come back to make sure they were safe and to swim back to the rest of the family with them.

Molly told her father the truth of what she had done. He was just as upset and disappointed as her mother had been. He said he would think about her punishment as they were swimming back to their family.

So, do you think Molly ever ate a whale hunter again, or swam off all by herself?

THE GREAT PURPLE MOUNTAIN

A PURPLE SPARKLE STORY

There once was a Great Purple Mountain. Beside this mountain there was a little village. Little Hanna lived in this village. It was a special village because it was a village of artists. Everyone there painted pictures. What was really special about this village of artists was that they painted with flowers. The flowers that grew in their gardens were magic flowers. The artists could paint with them. All they had to do was simply pick a flower out of the ground and they could use it like a paintbrush.

Now, the pictures all of the people painted were okay. They weren't great. They were just okay. Just average. Not really anything special. You see, no one had the color of purple to paint with. No purple flowers grew anywhere in the whole village. So, when someone was inspired to paint a beautiful picture using the color of purple, all of the villagers would just sigh and use a red color, or an orange, or a yellow, or a green, or a blue instead. And they settled for that. It was okay. Everyone understood there were no purple painting flowers that grew anywhere in the village, and everyone was okay with that. It's just the way it was.

In fact, no one in the village had ever before even wondered why there were no purple flowers growing in the village that they could paint pictures with. It's just the way it was – the way it had always been. The only purple flowers that grew anywhere were on the Great Purple Mountain. It was covered with all kinds of purple flowers. But no one had ever gone to the Great Purple Mountain and picked any of the purple flowers that grew there. They just looked at the Great Purple Mountain and sighed a sad sigh because they had no purple flowers that grew in the village.

So everyone would just settle for using other colors and forget all about using a purple color. Except for Little Hanna. She saw all of the beautiful purple flowers on the Great Purple Mountain and was not satisfied just using some other color instead. So if she painted a picture and there was supposed to be some purple in it, well, she just left that spot blank. Some of the villagers would get upset with Little Hanna because her pictures would sometimes be different from all of the other people's pictures.

Little Hanna liked to paint pictures of the Great Purple Mountain, so a lot of times there were blank spots in her pictures. Sometimes they were little blank spots, and sometimes they were big spots. When she was asked, "Why are there blank spots in some of your pictures? Why don't you finished your painting?" Little Hanna would answer, "Oh, that is a picture of the Great Purple Mountain. That blank spot is where purple would go, but I don't have purple, so it is a blank spot."

"Well, why don't you just use a different color to fill in that blank spot, like the rest of us do?" the other villagers would ask.

"Because it is the Great Purple Mountain and I want to paint it how it really is," Little Hanna would say. "Oh, I can't just use any old color, as pretty as they are. Only the color of purple is supposed to go there. But, since I don't have any purple flowers to paint with, it's a big blank spot."

Little Hanna thought and thought to herself, "I can't use red, or orange, or green, or blue when it's supposed to be purple. It may be okay for everyone else, but I want to paint the Great Purple Mountain how it really is. How, oh how, can I get any purple flowers to paint with?"

So Little Hanna did something that had never been done before. That night when she said her nightly prayers, she prayed for purple flowers. That's all. She prayed for purple flowers to paint with. And little did she know, that someone somewhere was watching that prayer go all the way up to heaven.

The eagle who lived on top of the Great Purple Mountain watched Little Hanna's prayer as it traveled. It was like a small, white wisp of smoke, gently floating up through the air. Eagle watched as Little Hanna's small little prayer came up, up, up, to the top of the Great Purple Mountain. Then Eagle watched the small little prayer go up, up, up, through the sky, and up, up, up, past the clouds all the way into heaven. And he followed it. He followed Little Hanna's prayer right into heaven.

God smiled and said, "Hello, my good friend Eagle. What a fine night it is for you to visit."

Eagle spread his mighty wings open wide and bowed to his best friend. "Yes Sir, a fine night indeed. I followed Little Hanna's prayer here tonight Sir."

"Ah, yes" said God, folding his hands together and putting them on his lap. "Little, little Hanna. A very wonderful and creative little girl! A perfect little girl in My eyes. A marvelous girl!"

"Yes Sir," replied Eagle. "I followed her prayer up to heaven tonight. It looked different than the other prayers I have seen come to You from the village. So, I wanted to see what it was and how You are going to answer it."

God laughed, and clapped his hands with joy. "It's happened Eagle! It's finally happened! Finally someone in the village has prayed for purple flowers! Oh, what a fine night in heaven this is indeed!" God got so excited that he tossed his friend Eagle way up into the air!

As Eagle flew back down, God continued. "Of course, the purple flowers have been on the Great Purple Mountain all along, but no one has asked for them until now! Everyone else in the village has been content to settle for just the colors they already have. But not sweet Little Hanna! She has had purple in her heart all this time. She just had to remember that. And tonight she has done it Eagle! She remembered that she could ask me for purple flowers! Yes, yes, it is a magically, sparkling night indeed!"

Eagle shook out his feathery wings and said. "Yes Sir, but there is something I don't understand.

Anyone in the village could have prayed for the purple flowers before now, but no one ever has. Why not? Why has everyone in the village settled for so long *not* having purple flowers to paint with? Everyone in the village is an artist. I don't understand why they are content to use a different color when they really want to use purple in their paintings. All of the people see the purple flowers growing on the Great Purple Mountain every day. Why don't they just go to the Great Purple Mountain and get them?"

"That's just it," answered God. "The people see the Great Purple Mountain every day. But they forget about the little purple flowers. They see a big mountain that they think is too far to get to. They see a big mountain that they think would be too hard for them to climb. They see a big mountain and believe they can never have the flowers that grow there. In fact, they think it is impossible to have purple in their lives at all. It is very sad."

"All they would have to do is ask for the purple flowers like Little Hanna has done, and believe in their hearts they that can have them," God said. "They could leave space for purple to be in their paintings like Little Hanna has done. She has the blank spots in her pictures because she knows that only the color of purple can fill them and make her paintings more than just okay. They would be beautiful. And, since Little Hanna has asked for purple she shall have it."

Eagle said, "I understand. But how are you going to get the purple flowers to Little Hanna? Sir, she really is much too little to climb up the Great Purple Mountain to get the purple flowers all by herself."

God smiled and said, "You mighty Eagle. You will bring the purple flowers to Little Hanna. While she sleeps, go back to the Great Purple Mountain and pick a purple flower for her to paint with. Set it on her windowsill so she will see it when she wakes up in the morning."

So that is just what Eagle did. While Little Hanna slept, that very night Eagle picked a purple flower from the Great Purple Mountain and placed it at her windowsill. The next morning when Little Hanna woke up and saw the purple flower on her windowsill what do you think she did? She ran to her paintings of the Great Purple Mountain and filled in the blank spots with the color of purple!

"Hooray!" Little Hanna exclaimed. "My prayer to have purple is answered!"

When all of the other villagers saw Little Hanna's Great Purple Mountain picture, they could hardly believe it. "How? How did you do it? Where did you get a purple flower to paint with?" they asked.

"I prayed for it," she answered. "I prayed for purple last night, and this morning a purple flower was lying on my windowsill."

"Do you think anyone in the village could pray for purple flowers to paint with?" asked one of the villagers.

"Of course you can! Everybody can," answered Little Hanna.

So that night when all of the villagers said their prayers, they each prayed for a purple flower to paint their paintings with. And the very next morning there were purple flowers growing in every yard in the village. God didn't just give each one of them a single purple flower – He gave them all entire gardens of them.

And it all started with one little girl who left blank spots in her paintings, and prayed for a purple flower.

CODY BUG BUTTERFLY AND IT IS

A PURPLE SPARKLE STORY

"Do it again! Do it again!"

Some of the little caterpillars were watching Mavis Butterfly do flying back flips in the air. Yep, Mavis Butterfly. Good 'ol Mav. Mavis Butterfly could do anything. Flying front flips. Flying back flips. She could fly in sideways circles! All of the caterpillars liked to watch Mavis Butterfly do her flying butterfly tricks.

All of them except Cody Bug Caterpillar. He was not having anything to do with part of it.

"Someday you will be able to do this too!" said Mavis Butterfly to all of the little caterpillars. "Nope, not me," Cody Bug Caterpillar replied. "I'm perfectly happy just being a caterpillar, thank you very much."

"Well, it is what it is," said Mavis Butterfly. "All caterpillars grow up to be butterflies when their Sleep Day comes. You will, too."

"Nope. Not me," said Cody Bug Caterpillar.

When The other caterpillars would reminded him, "Yeah Cody Bug, it is what it is. We all grow up to be butterflies when our Sleepy Day comes and we curl up inside our cocoons." But Cody Bug Caterpillar would simply always reply, "Nope. Not me. Who would want to be a dumb old butterfly anyway?"

But the truth was Cody Bug Caterpillar really did want to be just like Mavis Butterfly. He wanted to do flying front flips, flying back flips, and fly in sideways circles. He just didn't want to go through the hard and scary part of becoming a butterfly.

The scary part. The lonely part. The dark place part.

"Aw, come on" said one caterpillar. "It can't be all that bad. Just look at all the butterflies we know who used to be caterpillars. Mavis Butterfly says, 'It is what it is, and that all caterpillars grow up in their cocoon and turn into butterflies.' If they all did it we can do it, too!"

But Cody Bug Caterpillar was too frightened to even think about becoming a butterfly. He didn't want to build a cocoon.

He didn't want to have to change to become a butterfly. And most of all he did NOT want his Sleepy Day to come. The inside of his cocoon would be the darkest dark, ... and he would be all alone. Oh! Just thinking about the Sleepy Day made his stomach all gurgly and his head all dizzy. He kept thinking about what Mavis Butterfly said: "It is what it is."

"What in the world is she talking about?!" Cody Bug thought to himself. "What is 'It is what it is it'? I don't get it. But Mavis Butterfly is happy, and she does do some pretty cool tricks. so I don't know. I just don't know."

Just then an idea came to Cody Bug Caterpillar. What if he learned to fly without becoming a butterfly? Hmmm. He hung onto two leaves and flapped them as he jumped off a small tree branch. He "flew" for about a second, then fell the rest of the way and got a face full of mud when he hit the ground. He tried to fly again using two small bird feathers he had found. But the result was the same. Again, all he got was a face full of mud, added with a tiny bit of bird feather stuck in his mouth. Yuck.

Over the next few days, Cody Bug Caterpillar watched as all of the other caterpillars began to yawn and, one by one, curl up into their cocoons when it was their Sleepy Day.

But Not Cody Bug Caterpillar, though! Nope! Not him! Curling up into that dark and lonely cocoon all by himself and changing into a butterfly!--- was just too scary to even think about!

But as it is with all caterpillars, the day came when Cody Bug Caterpillar began getting more tired than usual. "Well, I could build a cocoon just to see what it looks like," he told himself. "I don't have to get into it and go to sleep."

Mavis Butterfly flew by as he was building his cocoon. "Nice cocoon!" she said. "I guess you are getting ready for your Sleepy Day?"

"Nope," said Cody Bug Caterpillar, with a big yawn. "Not me. I just wanted to see what my cocoon would look like." Mavis Butterfly smiled as she flew away. "Well it is what it is," she said. "All little butterflies have their Sleepy Day, curl up in their cocoon and wait to become a butterfly."

Cody Bug Caterpillar worked and worked and worked and built his own cocoon. When Cody Bug Caterpillar was finished, making his cocoon, he was very tired. It was then that he realized he had a little bit of a problem: it was the darkest dark inside his cocoon, and he hadn't leave left an opening in the cocoon so he could get out! And now he was starting to feel afraid and lonely inside the cocoon! Yep, he had a problem.

"Well, as Mavis Butterfly would say, 'It is what it is,'" he thought to himself with a big yawn. he said, "Maybe I could just take a short nap. That was hard work building my cocoon! I'll just take a short nap, then undo part of the cocoon and crawl out. I sure don't want to fall asleep and wake up being a butterfly! So what if I can't do a front flip or a flying back flip? And so what if I can't fly in sideways circles? Nope, not me! I think staying a caterpillar is just fine."

Cody Bug Caterpillar yawned a big yawn and curled up in his cocoon for a short nap. Then it happened! Cody Bug Caterpillar's Sleepy Day had arrived. He slept and slept and slept. He slept for days and days and days. And while he was sleeping, he had dreams.

He dreamed that he was trying to do a flying back flip and he crashed to the ground. He tried to do a front flying flip, but all he could only do was a somersault. And when he tried flying in a sideways circle, he hit a tree. Even in his sleep Cody Bug Caterpillar did not want to be a butterfly.

But then he heard a voice calling his name. A real voice, not one in his dream! He wasn't dreaming this sound. He could hear sound of his own name being called! He woke him up to the sound of "Cody…Cody Bug…."

Cody Bug Caterpillar He stood up quickly and said, "Uh, hello? Who's there?"

"It's me," the Voice replied. "I am, It Is, your Creator."

"Oh! You are the It Is? You created me? Mavis Butterfly talks about you all the time, but I never understand what she means," said Cody Bug Caterpillar. "Where are you? It is so dark in here that I can't see anything. This is really scary!"

"Don't be afraid," said the Voice of It Is. "I am here in the darkness with you. There is nothing for you to be afraid of, I promise."

"But what are you doing here, and how did you get in here?" asked Cody Bug Caterpillar.

The Voice softly answered, "Oh, my sweet little caterpillar. I am everywhere. It is very easy for me to be in your cocoon. That is part of me being It Is. I can be everywhere. I am here with you, inside your cocoon with you, to help you grow and turn into a butterfly."

Cody Bug Caterpillar looked all around him. He even squinted his eyes to help him see better, but it was dark as darkest dark inside his cocoon. "Nope. Not me," he said as he was looking looked all around in the darkness. "I don't want to be a butterfly, thank you very much."

"Why not?" asked the Voice. "You will be a beautiful and strong butterfly. You will bring much happiness and peace to everyone who sees you, just by being yourself around them. Butterflies are one of my favorite creations."

Cody Bug shook his head in the dark, and said, "I am afraid I won't be able to do a flying front flip."

"I know," the Voice responded.

"And I am afraid I won't be able to do a flying back flip."
"I know."

"And mostly I am afraid of not being able to do flying sideways circles."

"I know, and I will be right there with you to help you do those things when it is time to do them."

Cody Bug Caterpillar thought about that for a second, then said, "Nope. Not me. Thanks all the same, but I have never been a butterfly before and I am very scared to be one."

Cody Bug finally gave up on trying to see through the darkness and sat back down.

"Well," said the Voice, "You know, I could have created you to be anything in the whole world.

But creating you to be a butterfly was my best plan for you. You being Cody Bug Caterpillar was part of my best plan for you. Were you afraid to be a caterpillar?"

"No. I like being a caterpillar very much," answered Cody Bug.

"Have you ever had a not scary thought about being a butterfly?" asked the Voice.

"Well, yeah," said Cody Bug. "I like watching Mavis Butterfly do all of her butterfly tricks." It Is smiled at the little caterpillar. "Cody Bug, if you like being a caterpillar,

THE SPARKLES IN ME

can you trust me that growing and turning into a butterfly is my best plan for you? It's better than staying a caterpillar. And I promise I will always be right with you for the rest of your butterfly life?"

Cody Bug Caterpillar took in a deep breath and let it out slowly. Then he said, "Okay, I trust you. Make me a butterfly." And with a big, BIG yawn, Cody Bug Caterpillar fell fast asleep. While he was asleep, It Is worked a miracle like no one else can. He turned Cody Bug Caterpillar into Cody Bug Butterfly.

When the day came that Cody Bug woke up, he took down part of his cocoon, stepped out onto a tree branch, and stretched his new butterfly wings wide. He took in a big breath of fresh spring air. Just then Mavis Butterfly flew by. "Why Cody Bug Caterpillar! Is that you? What a beautiful butterfly you have turned into!"

Cody Bug flapped his new butterfly wings. "Yep! It's me! Watch this!" He flew up, up, up into the air and did a flying front flip, a flying back flip and – yes! – he even flew in a sideways circle. shouting, "It Is what it is and I am Cody Bug Butterfly!" he shouted.

Then he heard the Voice of It Is, his creator. "Hello Cody Bug. How do you like being a butterfly?"

Cody Bug did another flying front flip and answered, "I love it! This sure was a great plan you had for me!"

"And are you afraid anymore?"

Cody Bug Butterfly stretched out his wings and answered, "Nope. Not me! I know you changed me from a caterpillar into a wonderful butterfly, and I know you will always be with me."

"You are absolutely right," said It Is. "Now, show me one of those great Cody Bug Butterfly flying sideways circles."

So Cody Bug Butterfly did just that.

HAROLD IMAGINER AND THE PURPLE SPARKLES

A PURPLE SPARKLE STORY

"Okay everybody! Get ready! Let's get to work! The children will be asleep soon!" That was Stanley Imaginer. Stanley Imaginer was is charge of all the Imaginers. He was the boss. Imaginers are the ones who send all the Purple Sparkles full of creative and wonderful ideas into children's dreams at night. Imaginers are very important beings. Stanley Imaginer was getting his workers ready to go to work. Stanley loved being the boss.

He thought nothing was as important as being the boss. Millions and millions of Imaginers stood by their Purple Sparkle launching machines and got ready to launch Purple Sparkles full of creative and wonderful ideas into the night sky. There were sling shoters (shot-ers), and catapults. There were rocket racers, feathery floaty flippers and bouncy balloon droppers, and many other kinds of machines ready at the launch line.

James Imaginer was about to start his count down to launch, like he did every night. James Imaginer loved saying the count down. He thought nothing was as important as saying the count down.

"Ready Imaginers!" said James through his microphone. "5 – 4 – 3 -". "Wait! Wait! Don't finish that countdown!". That was Paisley Imaginer. She came running up to Stanley Imaginer and said, "Stop the countdown. Sir, we have a problem." Paisley Imaginer was in charge of quality control and she loved her job. She thought nothing was as important as quality control on the launch line.

"What is it?" asked Stanley Imaginer.

As Paisley Imaginer tried to catch her breath she said, "You gotta get Harold Imaginer off of sling shoter #7, Sir. Last week he mis-aimed. He accidentally hit a families' cat with a Purple Sparkle full of creative and wonderful ideas. A cat, Sir! The cat dreamed it could fly and sing like a bird! Fly, Sir! Like A bird, Sir! The cat woke up, climbed a tall tree and started screeching to high heaven, thinking it was singing like a bird! It woke up all the neighbors, Sir. They had to call the fire department to get the cat down out of the tree when it figured out it couldn't fly! It took hours! Was a complete disaster, Sir! You gotta do something!"

"Okay, okay," said Stanley Imaginer. "Let's put Harold Imaginer on a bouncy balloon dropper for tonight and see how he does." "You got it Sir!" said Paisley Imaginer, with a thumbs up. And off she went to move Harold Imaginer away form sling shoter #7 and put him on bouncy balloon dropper #42. "Maybe we should have a safety meeting before work tomorrow night," said Stanley Imaginer.

"It is very important to get the right Purple Sparkle full of creative and wonderful ideas to the right child. It could be a problem if a child is dreaming a dream that really isn't theirs. And we certainly don't need any cats acting like birds."

Well that perked up the ears of Matty Imaginer! He was in charge safety at the launch line. He loved scheduling safety meetings! He didn't think there was anything more important than safety at the launch line. "I will schedule a safety meeting for first thing tomorrow night, Sir!" he said as he ran off to his office to get an ink pen.

James Imaginer cleared his throat. "May I PLEASE start the count down now?!" Stanley Imaginer gave him an 'ok' sign. James Imaginer picked up his microphone and said into it, "5-4-3-2-1-0 LAUNCH!"

Instantly millions and millions of Purple Sparkles full of creative and wonderful ideas filled the night sky!

Millions and millions of Sling shoters, feathery floaty flippers, rocket racers, catapults, bouncy balloon droppers and many other kinds of machines launched them off the launch line, through the night sky, and right into the minds of millions and millions of children as they slept.

Shouts and applause came from the launch line. "Great job everyone! Now go home and get some rest. Be here a little early tomorrow night for a safety meeting," said Stanley Imaginer. As all the Imaginers were leaving the launch line, Harold Imaginer patted some of them on the back and shook their hands, saying, "Don't we have the greatest job in the whole world! Great job tonight everyone! Whoo -wee I love this job! See you tomorrow night everyone!" Harold Imaginer was always happy and he was always encouraging the other Imaginers. He thought nothing was more important than encouraging others. At the safety meeting the next night, Paisley Imaginer spoke to Stanley Imaginer. "Sir, we are going to have to do something about Harold Imaginer. I know he means well, and he is very encouraging to all the launch line workers, but-"

"Okay. Okay. What happened?", asked Stanley Imaginer. "Didn't you put him on a bouncy balloon dropper at the launch last night? That's one of the easiest machines to operate that we have."

Paisley answered quietly, "Well, yes Sir. Yes, I did. And well Sir, he uh – he – uh. He 'passed gas' Sir." "What? He did what? Speak up." said Stanley Imaginer.

Paisley Imaginer let out a sigh and said frantically, while she waved her arms in the air, "Farted Sir! He farted! Harold Imaginer farted as he was launching the bouncy balloon dropper and well, Sir, some of the stink got on the Purple Sparkle he was launching. It was bad, Sir. Really bad! The stink hit the Purple Sparkle and caused it to change direction. It hit a mom, Sir. A Mom!. She dreamed the whole house was full of rotten eggs, Sir! She made the whole family spend the whole day cleaning the whole house because she couldn't get the stink smell out of her head, Sir. No one in that family had any creative or wonderful ideas or fun today, Sir. It was really bad! You have gotta do something!"

"Okay, okay. Calm down. I will talk to Harold Imaginer and see what solution we can come up with." said Stanley Imaginer.

"Thank you, Sir," said Paisley Imaginer, sniffling a little bit. "I, I just can't take another mistake like that, Sir. Who knows who or what Harold will hit next time." Then Paisly Imaginer walked away, shaking her head and saying to herself, "He farted, he actually farted on the launch line. Never in my life-"

So, Stanley Imaginer called Harold Imaginer into his office. "Harold, I have had a couple of complaints about your launches lately. Can you tell me what is going on?" Harold Imaginer's face turned a little red. "Oh, the bouncy balloon dropper. Last night. Oh, that. I had hot dogs with stinky cheese for dinner yesterday, Sir. I am real sorry. It won't happen again. I just get so excited seeing all the Purple Sparkles filled with creative and wonderful ideas ready to get launched into the night sky. I am just so proud of all of the workers at the launch line I can hardly stand it! I guess I got a little too excited last night, and then, well I guess you know what happened. I am real sorry Sir."

Stanley Imaginer walked to his chair behind his desk and sat down. "Well, it isn't just last night. Last week you made a cat think he could fly and sing like a bird Harold, and well, that can just cause a lot of problems for everybody."

Harold Imaginer lowered his eyes to the floor. "Yes, Sir. I understand." he said.

Stanley Imaginer sat behind his desk and thought for a minute and then he got a big smile on his face. He said, "Harold Imaginer, I like you. I like you a lot. I have noticed that of all the Imaginers, you seem to be happy and encouraging to others. I also have noticed that at the end of every work night, you are always telling all of the other Imaginers that they have done a good job. That's very special, and important. "But, we simply can not have mistakes on the launch line. It is so important that just the right Purple Sparkles full of creative and wonderful ideas get to the right children's minds as they sleep. I am going to have to pull you off of the launch line, Harold. So, I have created a new position on the launch floor, and you , Harold Imaginer, will be the first Imaginer to have it."

"Wow! Really Sir? Thank you!" said Harold Imaginer.

Then Stanley Imaginer pulled out a bright, sparklely vest. It had Harold Imaginer's name on the front. And, on the back, in big bright, sparklely letters it said, 'Chief Encourager.' "From now on Harold Imaginer, your job will be to do just what you love to do. You are the best Encourager I know. So I want you to wait at the door when our workers come to work and leave from work, and keep telling them they are doing a good job, and that their work here is very important. Because it is."

Harold Imaginer was so excited he stood up and saluted! "Yes, Sir. You can count me, Sir! Chief Encourager Harold Imaginer reporting for duty Sir!" Stanley Imaginer chuckled, "Okay, Okay. Just one thing. Stay COMPLETELY away from the launch line. No more singing cats or rotten egg dreams."

"Yes Sir! Will do, Sir!" said Harold Imaginer. And he saluted again. Then Harold Imaginer went to work. He loved being the Chief Encourager. He thought there was nothing more important than being Chief Encourager.

So, the next time you wake up from a creative and wonderful dream, remember the Purple Sparkle that you have inside your mind and the Imaginer who put it there. And remember Harold Imaginer, so you can be a chief Encourager too.

CHARTS AND RESOURCES

JORETTA LUREE VETOR

SPARKLE STONES

PURPLE – Amethyst, Purple Agate, Purple Tourmaline

BLUE – Sodalite, Blue Sapphire, Blue Agate

GREEN – Emerald, Jade, Aventruine

YELLOW – Tigers Eye, Pyrite, Citrine

ORANGE – Camelian, Fire Opal, Orange Jasper, Topaz

RED – Garnet, Ruby, Red Jasper

THE SPARKLES IN ME

THE "I" CHART

Purple...I think
Blue... I say
Yellow...I can
Green... I have
Orange...I know
Red... I am

MUSIC:

THE KEYS AND FREQUENCIES

Remember I have combined the purples in my sparkles and me program. Both frequencies and music keys will work for the purple sparkle.

Music soothes the savage beast, they say. It is true. We all know that different music makes us feel different ways. You can use the specific frequency of each color to help with each Sparkle. This is great for mediation or "sleep music." For example, if you and your child are working with their green Sparkle, find a piece of music on YouTube that is in the 512 frequency and let it play while they are sleeping.

There are thousands of pieces of music on YouTube to choose from. Simply type in the frequency number and the word "music" into the search box and look at see the results. I have kept this list simple here.

Each Sparkle color naturally resonates with a KEY of music. A musical note. Also each color vibrates to a specific frequency. Here is a chart to help you. Use this as a tool for picking music that to listen to that correlates to whichever

Sparkle you are working with at the time. The keys of B and A can both be used for the Purple Sparkle.

• Purple – crown, third eye, top of head, forehead – Key of B and A. Frequencies: is 864Hz and 576Hz

• Blue – throat – Key of G. Frequency: is 768Hz

• Green – heart – Key of F. Frequency: is 512Hz

• Yellow – solar plexus – just above belly button – Key of E. Frequency: is728Hz

• Orange – sacral – just below belly button – Key of D. Frequency: is 1212Hz

• Red – base – Key of C. Frequency: is 912Hz

Music Chakra Chart:

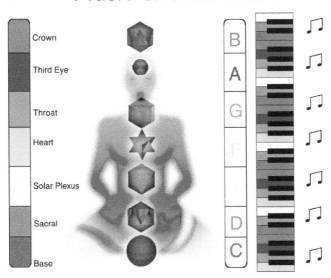

BIBLE VERSES

IN FIRST PERSON

I believe Ecclesiastes 3:11, "God has made everything beautiful for its own time. He has planted eternity in the human heart, but even so, people cannot see the whole scope of God's work from beginning to end."

This speaks volumes to me. Color is universal and eternal. Put God's Words about color into your child. It will serve them well their whole life. This simple Bible verse game will help and it is fun. Remember to reward, reward, reward! I chose the KJV simply for wording.

RED – Philippians 4:13, "I can do all things through Christ which strengthens me."

Sparkles version ... (Child's name) can do anything because Jesus makes me strong.

ORANGE – Psalms 46:10, "Be still and know I am God."

Sparkles version ... God says for (child's name) to be still and not afraid, and trust Him.

YELLOW – Proverbs 1:5, "A wise man will hear and will increase learning."

Sparkles version ... (Child's name) will hear, and listen, and will learn even more!

GREEN – II Timothy 1:7, "God has not given us a spirit of fear, but of power, and of love, and of a sound mind."

Sparkles version ... God says that (child's name) does not have to be afraid or angry, because He gave me a great mind and a good heart.

BLUE – Ephesians 4:15, "But speaking the truth in love, may grow up into him all things."

Sparkles version ... (Child's name) can say the truth all the time. It helps me grow big and strong.

PURPLE – Jeremiah 29:11, "For I know the plans I have for you, declares the Lord, plans to prosper you and not to harm you, plans to give you a hope and a future."

*Sparkle*s version ... God has great plans, and hopes and dreams for (child's name).

THE LORD'S PRAYER

SPARKLE STYLE

PURPLE
Our Father, which art in heaven, Hallowed be thy Name.
BLUE
Thy Kingdom come.
YELLOW
Give us this day our daily bread. And forgive us our trespasses, As we forgive them that trespass against us.
GREEN
Thy will be done on earth as it is in heaven.
ORANGE
And lead us not into temptation, But deliver us from evil.
RED
For thine is the kingdom, The power, and the glory, For ever and ever. Amen

PSALM 23

SPARKLE STYLE

Purple
The Lord is my shepherd, I lack nothing.
Blue
He makes me lie down in green pastures, he leads me beside quiet waters,
Yellow
Even though I walk through the darkest valley, I will fear no evil,
for you are with me; your rod and your staff, they comfort me.
Green
He refreshes my soul.
He guides me along the right paths for his name's sake.
Orange
You prepare a table before me in the presence of my enemies. You anoint my head with oil; my cup overflows.
Red
Surely your goodness and love will follow me all the days of my life,
and I will dwell in the house of the Lord forever.

MY STORY

We were playing the same 'picking up toys' game we always played. My five year old son was picking up his toys by color. I watched him thoughtfully pick up all the red toys, then his green toys and so on, and put them into the toy box. Only the blue toys were left to be put away. I said, "OK, now pick up your blue toys and put them in the toy box." Instead of picking up his blue toys, my son did something that forever changed our lives. He solemnly looked at me and said, "Mommy, I don't see my blue toys today."

He was not being defiant. This was a very obedient and pleasant little boy. He seemed genuinely troubled at this revelation of his non-existent blue toys. In that instant, it felt like lightning had struck our house. He was saying something much more profound than "I don't see my blue toys today." And I had a very good idea what it was and why he said it. I knew in that instant that COLOR was the way I could communicate with my son.

To avoid going into awful and dramatic details, I will give you a brief history of what led us up to that moment. My son had already been through many traumatic events by age five: breathing and eating problems since birth, heart surgery for a rare birth defect at age 2, living through some pretty horrible circumstances and a nasty divorce and custody battle that left my son and I separated for almost two years. When all the horrible events were over and we were finally permanently and safely reunited, he was left understandably traumatized. Even though he was back with me, I felt like he wasn't the same little boy. He had been through too much for such a young age. He simply couldn't talk about some things that bothered him or that he had nightmares about.

When the words, "I can't see my blue toys today" came out of his mouth, I knew this was the way I could start to communicate with him and to help him be happy again, help him be himself again.

I had studied the chakra system for quite a while, and I knew that the BLUE chakra was in the throat and that it deals with TRUTH and EXPRESSION. It made perfect sense that he "couldn't see" his blue toys. There were painful things he could not talk about. He could not express or "see" his truth. Almost thirty years ago, there were not as many tools to learn about the chakra system in the United States as there are today. So I was basically on my own. The Sparkles In Me was born out of desperation and the agony of watching my son be so frustrated and frightened. I color coded his world with the chakra colors, combining the purples together for simplicity's sake. I developed games and everyday practical ways to instill and talk about the chakras on his five year old level. I saw results quickly in his behavior and confidence and his sense of security. It just got better from there.

When my next son was born, I noticed at nine months old, that there was something not quite right. He angered so easily. He crawled backwards. He developed his own language for common things. I joked that he was "as good as gold, as mean as a snake." By age two, his temper would just explode out of nowhere. He cried out of frustration. He would say things are "too loud," "too bright," "my brain won't be quiet." It was agony watching him just get though most days of his childhood.

He organized his toys in a line. He stashed hot wheel cars in his pillow case. He had no fear or sense of danger at all, which only got worse as he got older. He had all the signs of dyslexia and dyspraxia, again at the time, there was not much for in the way of resources from which I could glean.

So we home schooled, tried several times to get a correct diagnosis, counseling, and daily hung on for dear life. Most medications at the time were not helpful. (I will never say to not get help from professionals!) I never knew what he was going to do.

I have two sons. My oldest was the perfect child. He rarely had to be disciplined. But he was quite melancholy. He needed his spirits lifted a lot of the time. My youngest was a handful to say the very least. With *The Sparkles In Me* again I found a way to help him communicate, cope with things, and keep our life progressing in a good way. But trust me, there were lots of days when I thankfully prayed, "Well, he didn't break anything, hit his brother, or climb out on the roof today." Again, I color coded his whole life.

The teenage years were fairly typical teen age years for both of my sons. One was never in trouble. One was in trouble a lot. Our lives were never easy. But I never lost faith or hope in either of them. We faced tragic times and good times together. I believe at the root of our relationship was this unspoken code of who we were. I taught my children from early on to "Remember who you really are." I kept believing that no matter if we drifted apart or didn't see eye to eye or no matter what direction our separate lives would take us, that we have a bonding cord, a knowing of each other, a way of communicating.

It is largely because of The Sparkles In Me that I have peace. We put the work in through the years and that is what it takes. Living daily with this teaching as a way to communicate with my sons, and now with my grandchildren, brings peace. It provides building blocks that we can go back to over and over and over and use to talk about things and understand each other.

This year my sons are ages 34 and 29. They are both pretty terrific guys. They use The Sparkles In Me with their own children. Our lives are very colorful and sparklely!

My utmost desire and prayer for you and yours is that The Sparkles In Me helps you in the same way. It is a magical and fun way to live. It gives so much meaning to the simplicities of life.

May you find The Sparkles in you and the fantastic children in your life. God bless.

FINAL THOUGHTS

I encourage you to keep a journal of the progress you see while using *The Sparkles In Me*. I still like to go back and read and remember the accomplishments, adventures, and milestones my children and I had. Once you have The Sparkles In Me in your life, things will never be the same. You will never look at or think of, colors as you once did. You will be amazed. I know I was. I believe you will see all color differently and appreciate more how God uses color in our world. And that will make you smile.

Here are a few tidbits from The Sparkles In Me from a few of the kids in my life and from my sons when they were younger.

Trenton, the oldest, was in first grade. One day he was nervous about his spelling test at school, so he asked if he could have a glass of water with some yellow power in it. I put a drop of yellow food coloring in a small cup of water and he drank it right up. The confidence that gave him was instantly shining on his face. He got a happy face from his teacher on that spelling test for getting all the words correct. That paper went on the fridge!

I loved when my boys would tell me of their Sparkle color dreams. They were always excited for the next one, and it made bedtime easier! At bedtime I would ask them what color they wanted to dream about. One night Dakota wanted to dream about Blue. He picked a blue boat, a blue puppy, and a blue castle. He was going to go to the blue castle to rescue a princess. The next morning when we talked about his dream, he was not very happy about it. I asked him what was wrong. "Well, my puppy didn't want to leave the big castle when it was time to go, so now tonight in my dream I have to go back and get him! He's kind of a bad dog!"

One of my favorite students I worked with was a little fourth grade boy, I will call him Malachi for this writing. He was more than a handful. I was assigned to help him in school and assess him. He had already been through several assistants and no one could handle him. He could get pretty violent with other students and teachers alike. It was my job to come up with and help him with an individual learning plan to help him. Malachi had a lot of rage. He scared the other students in his class so much at the beginning of our time together, that he could not last very long in the classroom in one sitting. More often than not it was necessary that we left the classroom and did our own learning sessions together in the library or outside.

When we walked in the hallway and a class of students was coming down the hall in our direction, I had to bodily shield him from attacking the other children. You can imagine what our school days were like! Malachi didn't talk much unless he was screaming. It was obvious how frustrated he was, but no one seemed to be able to get through to him. I was determined to unlock that frustration in his brain and give him a voice.

I cut 3x5 cards in half. I colored one in each of the Sparkle colors and laminated them. I put them all on a huge key ring, big enough that Malachi could put in on his wrist. When he would tell me something that was a lie, like telling me he had done his homework when he did not do it, he would tell me the lie, smile and then hold up the blue card. Then I would say, "Well, I will just wait for the blue truth answer." That was our start to what developed in a wonderful teacher/student friendship.

I cried the day I saw him, all on his own, pull out his GREEN card and, with outstretched arm, hold it up, arm stretched out at his side, and hold the card there, like a shield, facing a class of students who were walking toward us in the hallway. After the class had passed us with no outburst from Malachi, he whispered out loud but to himself, "I did it!" Yes, I cried. He had used his Green Sparkle to stay calm. We immediately celebrated with ice cream sandwiches in our little classroom.

At the end of a few weeks Malachi could last most of the day in the classroom and had made several friends. He was the class clown, so we worked out a deal with the teacher. For every hour and a half that he could stay in his seat and not disrupt class, Malachi got to stand in front of the class and tell a joke. Each time he would hold his key chain in his hand with the green card on top.

Dakota, my youngest son, had severe dyslexia. In the early '90s there were not the tools out there to help kids and parents like there are today. That is why I developed the colored alphabet. We made thousands of words out of play dough so he could see and feel the letters. The first time Dakota actually read the word "the," we were driving through town. He saw the word 'the' on a billboard. All of a sudden he shouted, "Mom! The! The!"

"The what?!" I asked.

He shouted because he was so excited. "Noooooo! I see the word THE!" We had been making his th's, ch's and sh's with blue play dough and the word "the" on the billboard was blue. I saw the light bulb go on in his mind. I saw the floodgates open. He could read!

I filled the truck up with gas and we drove all over town looking for the word "the." It was a breakthrough moment in his young life. He was eight years old. When we got home he wanted to read and sing the words to his favorite song, Kid Rock's "Only God knows Why." I printed out the words, turned on the stereo, hooked up Dakota's little microphone and he sang his heart out as he read the words. He probably sang it a dozen times in a row. It was a very special day.

Our miracles started happening that fall day when Trenton said, "Mommy, I don't see my blue toys today." I could share so many more personal stories with you but this tool kit isn't about me and mine. It is about you and the glorious children in your life. Go make some miracles happen. Learn to see the Sparkles in you and them. It will make you smile.

God bless,

JoRetta Luree

REAL LIFE EXAMPLE

This is an example of a typical gingerbread man session. I asked the same question to two children ages (child one) 11 and (child two) 8. As always we started with drawing the Sparkle Colors inside of the gingerbread man , all stacked up correctly.. This reassures the child that the Sparkle Colors are always there, even though we may not feel them there. They are always there, in their correct spots, because we are made perfectly.

The children each have a school subject that is very difficult for them. It is not pleasant or easy for them to talk about. To get to core of the issue, the gingerbread man helps tell their stories. Child #1 has difficulty with reading. Child #2 has difficulty with math.

To child #1 I asked, "When you know you have to read in school, where do you feel your Red Sparkle?" and so on, until we had spoken about all the Sparkle Colors and Child #1 drew them according to where they were when it comes to reading for school.

REMEMBER THERE ARE NO WRONG ANSWERS The child is telling me through where their heart, brain, and emotions are regarding the school subject.

1. Where do you feel your Red Sparkle, your physical energy, when you have to (read, do math) in school?

2. Where do you feel your Orange Sparkle, your wise decision making, when you have to (read, do math) in school?

3. Where do you feel your Yellow Sparkle, your confidence in learning, when you have to

(read, do math) in school?

4. Where do you feel your Green Sparkle, your calmness, when you have to (read, do math) in school

5. Where do you feel your Blue Sparkle, your telling the truth about it, when you have to (read, do math) in school?

6. Where do you feel your Purple Sparkle, your creativity, when you have to (read, do math) in school?

The answers the children gave are enlightening. The Gingerbread Man sessions is designed for this to happen. The question can be any question. It doesn't matter. The colors help them speak. They "hide" behind the colors.

Good
Day

Child #1.

This child is natural athlete, is learning more self control, and is very artistic. My interpretation of her placement of the Sparkle Colors in answer to "...when you have to read in school." is as follows. The Quotes are from the child.

Red – This child is so angry and frustrated about having to read in school that they "just want to punch reading!"

Orange – This child felt like that "can't a wise decision about reading."

Yellow – This child didn't know why they put their Yellow where they did. Since Yellow has to do with learning , to me this placement tells me this child is willing to at least try. If there were no Yellow placement at all, this would indicate a 'giving up attitude.

Green – This child said, "This is no calm about reading in school!" Blue – this child said "Well, I truthfully want to kick reading!"

Purple – No purple at all. No feeling of creativity.

Child #2.

Child #2 This child struggles some physically, is learning to implement daily routines at home and is very creative in acting and singing.

Red - "Usually I am trying to control my anger (about math) in my head!"

Orange – This child didn't remember why they put their orange sparkle where they did. To me this placement says this child is afraid of making mistakes.

Yellow - "Because I am still trying to learn."

Green - "Because my legs and feet are always moving and that helps me stay calm."

Blue - "Because doing math makes me nervous and have butterflies in my stomach."

Purple – same answer as Blue

ABOUT THE AUTHOR

JoRetta Luree Vetor has a degree in social work and 30+ years of experience in parent-child communication as well as emotional training for kids. She is a licensed Chaplin and grief counselor. She lives in Northern Indiana with her husband Darrell.

CPSIA information can be obtained
at www.ICGtesting.com
Printed in the USA
JSHW011653030120
3343JS00003B/16

9 781722 408527